GW00760130

LIFE SCIENCE AND RELIGIONS

By the same author:

Birth Defects and Their Causes

LIFE SCIENCE AND RELIGIONS

Kieran Burns
University College, Galway

Philosophical Library

New York

Library of Congress Cataloging in Publication Data

Burns, Kieran, 1926-
   Life science and religions.

      Includes index.
      1. Religion and science—1946-.   I. Title.
   BL240.2.B875   1984   291.1'75   83-25035
   ISBN 0-8022-2415-6

Copyright, 1984, by Philosophical Library, Inc.
200 West 57th Street, New York, N.Y. 10019
All rights reserved

Manufactured in the United States of America

CONTENTS

List of Illustrations

Tables

INTRODUCTION

This investigation arose from research on stress. Eve was told in Genesis that she would bring forth children in congenital stress, pain or difficulty in childbirth. This was a result of the "fall" of Adam and Eve from a state of perfection to one of imperfection, in the Garden of Eden. The "fall" is described as original sin and means human development of intellect, self-consciousness and freedom to make decisions independently of God's will. Congenital stress has now been shown to be psychosomatic, as evidenced by a direct relation between blood levels of stress hormones in late pregnancy and duration of labor. The latter is a good indication of difficulty or stress in childbirth. Thus life science supports the concept of original sin, and research has provided evidence to corroborate it. Scientific evidence in favor of original sin is a unifying force among world religions and it underlines the imperfection of man, as implied by all religions.

Mary gave birth to Jesus (from Yeshua in Aramaic; meaning Yahweh or God is salvation) without congenital stress, according to tradition. This fits in with Islamic and Christian teachings that Mary was without sin. In Islam, however, original sin and the need for human salvation are not accepted, nor is the crucifixion of Jesus by some Moslems. Mary claimed at Lourdes, to Bernadette (Marie Soubirous), that she is the Immaculate Conception, born without original sin. In Christian teaching this exception was made by God since Mary was to give birth to Jesus, whose perfection personified his divine nature. According to Christianity Jesus was spiritually the son of God, though not conceived by normal physical means.

Buddhism states that being born, being ill, growing old and dying are all associated with stress and suffering. Measurement of stress hormones in our research, in relation to childbirth and to disease, provides, in life science, a counterpart to Buddhism. The Buddha was born, according to tradition without congenital stress, in the village of Lumbini in north India (now Nepal). Buddha, like Jesus, taught that we should care for the sick. He is quoted as saying, "He who would wait on me, let him wait on the sick". Hindu Avatars represent stages in creative evolution, from the viewpoint of life science. The Vedas (Knowledge) and the Bhagavad Gita are concerned with human development, mentality, and spirituality as well as with medicine.

The main teachings of Islam appear to be that there is one God, and there is justification for reciprocality in behavior, such as "an eye for an eye" and "a slave for a slave". There is also a question as to whether man was created instantly. Stress and suffering are not given much attention in Islam, so there is little to state here from this point of view. The main question which is discussed about Islam is whether this religion is compatible with Christianity, which it follows in time.

New approaches used in this book are as follows:
1. Principles of scientific observation form the basis for the present investigation. These require, above all, that truth

of observations be confirmed by two or more people, and that visible scientific evidence is provided where possible to support beliefs.

2. Eve was promised congenital stress or difficulty in childbirth. The question is whether this human condition has a psychological or psychosomatic basis and whether evidence indicates that it is fundamentally caused by human intellectual development. A psychosomatic cause is now supported by medical research, using levels of stress hormones.

3. The availability of measurable parameters of suffering or stress in diseases, as well as in childbirth means that life science is now a counterpart of Buddhism.

4. From the point of view of life science, the Avatars of Hinduism may be considered as representing stages in evolutionary creation.

5. Human development has been accompanied by the occurrence of birth defects. This biological parameter of human inperfection enhances our understanding of spiritual imperfection of man.

6. Psychological or psychosomatic factors have been evoked in healing. We have found that there is not a correlation between blood levels of stress hormones ACTH and cortisol, and immune processes, as reflected by phagocytosis and blood levels of immunoglobulins. This finding is evidence contrary to psychosomatics in normal healing.

7. Healing can apparently be supernatural or divine, and not understandable from a biological viewpoint. The scale of the problem, in the biology of "spiritual" healing, is similar to that of one step in evolutionary creation. Biological evidence of divinity or spirituality, such as healing, is considerably more complex and advanced than purely physical or astrological arguments. Scientifically the latter are primitive evidence for the existence of God.

8. Creative evolution has received support from comparative physiological and biochemical studies. We now know that

genes of the chimpanzee are 99% similar to those of man. Biological evidence is strongly opposed to "instant creation".

9. Virginal birth of a son requires formation of a Y chromosome prior to conception. Formation of a Y chromosome, for the conception of Jesus, would have been similar to the beginning of a new phase in evolutionary creation.

10. Trinity has different meanings, and the denial of one, in the Koran, does not necessarily deny the perfection or divine nature of Jesus. Trinity means three personalities or emanations (flowing out) of divine spirit, in Jesus, and the Holy Spirit, of God, in time and space. The trinity of the Koran means "three thirds" and is material.

11. Apparitions are now scientific since millions of people saw the apparitions in Cairo and many people took photographs of them. The apparitions in Cairo are considered to be of considerable importance. They were seen at Zeitun, on the roof of a church built at the request of the mother of Jesus.

The author has carried out rerearch on DNA and RNA, wound healing, pituitary tissue culture, effects of hormones on the uterus, fetal growth, congenital stress (difficulty of human labor), the pineal gland hormone — melatonin, chromosomes, phagocytosis, immunoglobulins and stress hormones in human diseases. Such a variety of medical research interests have facilitated the present study and made possible a coverage of the present subject with broad scope, but with simple concepts and principles.

Results of medical research, carried out by the author, and relevant to *Life Science and Religions*, have been described in lectures and conferences in Europe, the United States, the Middle East and Asia. The scientific report on congenital stress, the consequence of original sin, was written at Jum-Joom, a stone's throw from the reputed burial place of Adam and Eve, in Jeddah, Saudi Arabia, while the author was Professor at King Abdullaziz Medical College. The corresponding scientific communication was given in Rome, in 1977, at the 5th International Conference on Psychosomatic Medicine in Obstetrics and Gynecology.

Research on stress in childbirth is being continued by the author. Since this book has gone to print it has been shown that there is a direct relation between urinary VMA (vanylmandelic acid) levels in late pregnancy and the duration of labor. Also, VMA output is inversely related to fetal growth. This correlation is suggestive of stress inhibiting growth of the fetus and causing birth defects. Furthermore, urinary output of adrenaline in late pregnancy is directly related to the (subsequent) duration of labor, indicating involvement of human emotional stress in the genesis of suffering in childbirth.

Kieran Burns

ACKNOWLEDGMENTS

I wish to acknowledge use of abstracts from translations of the Bhagavad Gita by Swami Swarupananda, published by Swami Budhananda, President, Advaita Ashrama Mayavati, Pithoragarh, Himalayas and by W. Douglas P. Hill, published by Oxford University Press; translation of the Koran by Abdallah Yousuf Ali, published by the Call of Islam Society; the R.S.V. Interlinear Greek-English New Testament, translated by Alfred Marshall, published by Samuel Bagster and Sons, Limited, London: the Holy Bible, Revised Standard Version (London: Catholic Truth Society); the texts of Taoism, etc.

I should like to acknowledge abstracts from "When Millions Saw Mary" by Francis Johnston, published by Augustine Publishing Company, Devon and from "Our Lord's Mother Visits Egypt" by Pearl Zaki (Dar El Alam El Arabi).

CHAPTER 1

LIFE SCIENCE AND RELIGION

The study of "Life Science and Religion" provides, above all other subjects, understanding of themes relating man to God. Life science and religion concern respectively the material and invisible forms of life, the finite and infinite, the imperfect and the perfect. The imperfection of human creation is apparent in people of all nationalities, colors, races and religions. Susceptibility to disease and to suffering is universal. World religions involve, to a varied extent, man's physical and psychological imperfection. The intellectual development of man, and associated selfishness, materialism, and suffering, are fundamental in Chinese religions, Hinduism, Buddhism and Christianity. In contrast, some religions involve materialism, politics and legislation. The scientist approaches the relation between life science and religion without prejudice, as he approaches research. The comparative sanity of scientific dialogue is "devoutly to be wished" among peoples of different religions. This requires a general and broad education, as well as an open mind, which is essential in the search for truth.

1

Advances in medical research, and in knowledge of life science, show that religion and life science are now one, i.e. united. They are both about creation, human life, suffering and its prevention, physical and psychological healing, attitudes and treatment of others, mentality and behavior. Individual human knowledge is like human vision; it is derived from one point or position and is limited in angle and direction. Human knowledge of a physical science implies ignorance also. It implies "one-pointed concentration" and is finite in character. Life sciences are multidisciplinary in approach and advance our understanding. Only infinite or "universal knowledge" leads to complete understanding, compassion, tolerance, love and forgiveness. Similarly in world religions, a knowledge of their various principles and fundamentals increases understanding. Education should have universal knowledge and understanding as its objectives.

Life science is an ideal parameter for a central role in evaluation of scripture and for attainment of understanding of cultures, traditions and religions. The mentality of openness, understanding and compassion which develop from education in life science, including medicine, is particularly suited to study religion. This attitude has been singularly lacking in many people. Religion has in fact been brought down to a human level, where viewpoints have been affected by the self-awareness and self-righteousness of man. This character introduces bias in favour of one's own limited viewpoint. Such bias is natural since the initial and fundamental nature of man has been to see things only from his own limited point of view. In becoming educated and learning life sciences, we acquire a universal mentality involving the knowledge of different peoples, cultures, traditions and religions.

Life is the most important part of creation; man the most complex form of life, and his mind the most advanced of all species. In creation man acquired intelligence, knowledge and human mentality. He has characteristics which we attribute to God, such as love, understanding, mercy, truth and justice. All good qualities of man are finite. This finiteness contrasts with the qualities of the "Absolute" which are infinite and perfect. Man is imperfect in his finite nature, physically, chemically, biologically and psychologically. Physically man is limited in time, space and energy. Chemically, man is restricted in composition, reactions and genetic constitution. Biologically he is limited in the power and direction of his movements, in vision, hearing, sensation and ability to learn. His limitation of knowledge implies ignorance and lack of understanding. Psychologically man is imperfect in his self-awareness, self-interest and resulting selfishness; in his insufficient concern and love for others, in limitation of mind, goodwill, understanding, love and forgiveness.

It is appropriate to ask what relation exists between life science and religions. This relation includes conception, health, mental development, family and community relations, reproduction, morals, prevention and alleviation of suffering, survival and death. Different religions exhibit a considerable difference in their fundamental central principles and relevance to development of the specific character of man. This character is the "sapiens" of "Homo sapiens," the unique mental development of the human species. The relation between the individual and society is fundamental in development of the mentality of man, and is recognized in all societies. Religions are somewhat uneven in their references to attitude to one's neighbour, some religions omitting mention, or at least serious considerations, of human relations. In life science these are well established as fundamental in medicine, psychology, psychiatry and in determining the quality of life.

In life science the creation of man is of primary interest, human health of fundamental importance and intelligence the foundation stone of development of "Homo Sapiens." The role of the Creator and sustainer of man is central in religion, which relates to man's physical and mental health, as well as his intelligence and free will. Prevention of disease, healing, alleviation of suffering, compassion, and personal, family and community relationships are all important aspects of human life science as well as religion.

Development of human intelligence has exposed man to stress and suffering of many kinds. The primary importance of

3

the unique character of man means that religion, if it is to be meaningful, must deal with stress and suffering as a central theme, or at least as a basic issue. Methodology in life science is now available for measuring stress hormones as parameters of suffering. Advances in medical sciences, in knowledge of healing, and physiology of control of sensation, including pain, mean that we can study the compatibility of scripture and life science, and assess the relevance of sections from scripture to specifically human problems. Medical research findings now support scriptural claims concerning the implications of human mental development of man's mind and body. It was implied in scripture that human intelligence and knowledge would lead to stress in human birth, i.e. congenital stress. This has now been investigated and results support the scripture in Genesis — which is the basis for the Christian concept of "original sin."

It is difficult for a person who has knowledge and upbringing in only one religion to have an open mind in respect of another. In science, however, one is trained to examine various points of view and results from different experimental approaches. This is especially true at a research level and it leads one to consider findings and conclusions of other investigators. In religion, no such attitude prevails among the vast majority, especially the uneducated, and the main factor determining one's religion is parental decision. Education introduces reason and enlightenment into personal choice, where the freedom to choose exists.

Education is accompanied by development of ability for critical appraisal. Scientific advance provides standards for measurement of truth, in biological as well as physical sciences. Life science is a new and reasonable standard, or parameter, for measuring credibility of scriptures. Human life science, including physiology, biology and medicine, has not been used before now, as a standard for assessing world religions. Advances in human knowledge and understanding, and in communication are putting all religions to the test of truth, particularly concerning compatibility with human rationality and life science. The considerable biochemical evidence in

4

favor of human creative evolution, from comparative analytical data, renders scriptural allegations of instantaneous human creation of man even less credible than before.

The old and primitive belief in predestination tends to favor suffering and to militate against availing of medical aid. Life science and medicine are partners of the Creator in promoting survival of mankind, in improving man's physical state, in preventing imperfection and suffering and alleviating pain, disease and mental stress. Some religions involve man, physically, socially, medically and in his unique psychological development. Man's social conscience, geared to prevent and alleviate suffering, is associated particularly with Christianity. The rights of the individual are promoted more in Western societies than in others. There is now less infliction of human suffering, particularly psychological, in the West than elsewhere, and civilization seems within closer reach. Laws are being extended to protect the individual against psychological, as well as physical suffering.

Attitude is fundamental in religion. It is desirable that this should change from aggression through understanding, to love and forgiveness. Only learning, knowledge and understanding can lead to compassion, empathy, and love for people including one's "enemies."

Reason and emotions are the highest attributes of the human mind and lead towards knowledge, understanding, compassion and abolishment of suffering. Religion has dealt with the unknown and the invisible in the past; modern science explains many of the facets of former ignorance and man has reached a stage of considerable knowledge. The physical aspects of the human body are well understood. Physical and chemical changes of the human brain, the most complex part of creation, have been largely elucidated. Modern knowledge is considerable, not alone in the physical sciences but in the biological and medical fields. In the past many scientists came to question religion. Their science, however, was usually astrology and they were concerned with scriptures written against a background of early human development. Life science has made considerable progress in the twentieth century

and it is now possible to examine confidently the relation be
tween religion and life science. Some religions are more compatible than others with life science. Life science accepts conclusions based on reason rather than revelation and results
from a number of investigators rather than one. The principles
of life science are employed in the present investigation and
therefore there is limited reliance placed on individual revelation. The modern theory of creative human evolution is in conflict with belief in instant creation but there is a harmonious
relation between life science and religion in physical, psychological and spiritual healing.

Cultures of societies have become absorbed in some religions, so that it is impossible to distinguish between culture
and religion in scriptures. The practice of ascribing law-giving
to God includes the ten commandments of Christianity and the
laws of the Koran and of the Torah. In the Old Testament,
stoning to death was prescribed for adultery; similarly in the
Koran. In the New Testament the attitude has changed to
forgiving, and the practice of stoning ceases to be condoned.
The future could bring a reversion, as in Islam, or an extension of Western influence through spread of civilization, with
freedom and its associated risks. More members of homo "sapiens" may become sufficiently civilized for the "stones" to be
withheld. The enormity of suffering, inflicted in God's name,
makes one hope for a spread of the practice of Christian principles. Differences in religion seem to involve politics, as much
as if not more than religion. Especially lacking in primitive religion is an objective of universal love and peace.

It is difficult to persuade people that God did not urge reciprocity on man. If He did, He is not a peacemaker, but encourages aggression, and human suffering. It is not in the interests of the future of man that principles of retaliation be
promoted. What is termed "reciprocity" or "an eye for an eye"
may have been adequate for tribal survival. It must be abolished, as a principle, by modern man, who has human destruction readily available on a vast scale. Dissension and strife
should be abolished as a political, as well as scriptural, principle. Primitive people should be civilized, which means "to be

instructed in arts and refinements"; "advanced beyond the primitive savage state and reclaimed from barbarism." Universal civilization of man can be expected to lead to love of God and of one's neighbor.

One of the problems of world religions has been to describe God as near or distant, distinct from man or within him, punishing or rewarding, omnipotent in a moment — or in time, present everywhere or limited in space. In life science it is realized that one speaks of qualities of God, the Creator, rather than God as a person and that these qualities are infinite in God but limited in man. Is God absolute or infinite? Is there "one" God (in number)? Is God one? Is God "everywhere"? Is God omnipotent? God is accepted as infinite since the universe is spatially unlimited in space in human terms and knowledge. The infinity of God is not only spatial as material is, but relates to character — goodness, love, truth, justice and perfection. The omnipotence of God means that He has infinite physical power at His disposal, which He controls. In life science this meaning is qualified by adding "over time" or "during time" since creative evolution implies creation in time, and not "in an instant." Omnipotence is also qualified, as a divine property, by excluding the ability to be evil, or to commit sin, which are not possible for God.

"One" God, a number referring to God, is not acceptable to science as an unqualified description. The description "one God" is a purely human inadequate description of God. The number "one" means a single individual thing or person. One, as a number, implies limitations. "One" refers, as scientific description and number, to material things. It cannot relate to infinity. God is infinite in scientific language. Infinite means without end or limit, "greater than any quality that can be assigned," not limited by person or number; that which is without determinate bounds but which cannot possibly admit of bound or limit; the Absolute; the "Infinite Being of God." "God is One" means that God is not separated, as materials may be, but is united; this statement is compatible with scientific meaning, whereas one God (in number) is not.

Human potential for evil depends on man's intelligence and

7

resulting free will. Free will is now accepted to be a character of man. In other species behavior is governed by instinct, or "built-in" impulses and behavioral patterns.

Free-will implies knowledge and the ability to distinguish or discriminate between good and evil. In life science discrimination causes stress; in experimental animals it leads to increased blood levels of stress hormones. Human intelligence, self-consciousness and free-will determined "original sin." This "sin" or "turning away from God" is human independence of God, in decision the advance beyond the concept, and reality, of "predestination" and of instinctual determination of behavior. It caused imperfection due to human self-consciousness and resulting selfishness. It is the "turning away" from God's perfect and direct control, the "disobedience" of independence and free will.

Imperfection of man contrasts with perfection of our Creator. A principle of divine and human "creation" is that imperfection is a character of anything which is created. At a human level man is unable to create anything equal to his own mind. The human mind, created by God, is inferior to God's. Evolution contradicts the "omnipotence" of God in the instantaneous biological sense; evolution does not agree with instant creation of any human being; omnipotence over a length of time, is however, compatible with science. Life science cannot accept that Adam or Christ was created in an instant.

In some scriptures it is clearly stated that God could create a man in a moment of time. There is clear incompatibility between these scriptures and life science. Evolution is accepted by almost everyone with up-to-date knowledge of biology — there are probably less than one percent of scientists who do not accept evolution of man. Some scriptures allow compatibility between scripture and life science, i.e. in Genesis. The creation of Adam and Eve from clay is considered as an indication of their ultimate material origin, a summary of creation, rather than an instantaneous creation. Scriptures are generally accepted as inspired by God and written by man. God is considered to have inspired man with their content; it is accepted that there may be some human influence leading to minor degrees of imperfection. Science indicates that all scriptures have a human influence. Scripture and science were written against the background of limited human knowledge, especially of life science. The contribution of God to scripture in inspiration and revelation should be constant and compatible with reason, absence of error or contradiction. There must be consistency, with no change made, if the scripture is entirely attributable to God. Lack of consistency in a scripture, and alterations, with substitution of new verses, are in conflict with science. Scripture is understood in human terms, and written in man's language, which is inadequate in relating to God. The influence of man on the content of scripture is evident from the scientific content. Where there is something incompatible with scientific truth this is of human origin. For example, if God were quoted as saying that the heart does not pump blood, then the error is to be attributed to the human writer. The human element in inspiration and revelation involves human imperfection and becomes evident through scientific appraisal.

Congenital stress, according to tradition, did not accompany the birth of Buddha or Christ. Our research findings indicate a relation between mental stress hormones and the stress of childbirth. Modern findings on stress, and coping with it, show that suitable action in moderation is the proper antidote to stress. Buddhism and Christianity combine to highlight suffering and the appropriate or inappropriate courses open to man in relation to it; evasion, forbearance, prevention or cure according to belief. The process of healing is similar to creation; it aims at restoration from physical imperfection to perfection. When instantaneous it bears the stamp of divinity — in healing Christianity and life science are one.

Man has primary interest in pleasure and material things. An example of human self-consciousness and associated selfishness is the pleasure involved in human reproduction. It is evident that divine design of biology of reproduction was for procreation of children. The important biological principle is survival by propagation of the species. The general human attitude is in contrast to the divine, and is often contrary to

9

biological function. Destruction of human life, at any stage, is contrary to biological principles. Similarly, prevention or procreation of children by artificial means is contrary to the design of creation and to human survival.

Aggression and criminality have important implications for psychological medicine as well as physiology of behavior. Increased levels of some hormones and brain chemical transmitters have a marked effect on behavior and apparently contribute to aggression or docility. Male reproductive hormones have been shown to play an important part in aggressive attitudes. Blood levels of these hormones are increased in individuals who are aggressive. A problem exists about crime; its understanding and prevention. Experience is showing that unsuitable environment, inadequate parental influence, poor education and less than average intelligence contribute to crime. Many punitive regulations were enforced and accepted because it was believed they were God's will. The justification of punishment in some religions is on the basis of "divine command" contained in scripture. Scriptural recommendation of flogging, stoning to death, and cutting off limbs contrasts with Christian mercy and forgiveness. In some religions and associated societies reward is the key to motivation, rather than punishment, and man is acknowledged to have free will. Where punishment is the dominating influence, religion and politics are totalitarian in character.

Knowledge and understanding expose the cause of crime and help man to make an effort to rehabilitate "guilty" persons. The attitude of Christ to criminals and sinners was one of affection and forgiving. He stated that we should not judge one another but that we should love and forgive. Modern opinion agrees that imprisonment or punishment, as such, does not change mentality, attitude or tendency to crime. A medical approach is evidently more appropriate than the Old Testament one of "an eye for an eye" and "a tooth for a tooth." The latter attitude is based on hate and is primitive in character. Differences in human attitudes to aggression, suffering, mercy and forgiveness, present among different cultures, are reflected in scriptures. Further, some scriptures en-

10

courage the perpetuation of reciprocity in murder and aggression. The implication of their divine origin makes change and civilization difficult to promote.

Perfection is the most important and worthwhile objective for man. Only by aiming at perfection can this state be attained. Perfection cannot be achieved by objectives, whose goals have human characters, which are finite and imperfect. Perfection cannot characterize politics, which is of human origin and based on human principles.

There will not be universal peace, justice, truth, happiness, until the ideal of perfection is sought where alone it exists; in spirituality. Human values and imperfection still abide in primitive man, in whom aggression and reciprocation are accepted with scriptural support.

Reason, emotion and action were designed for man's welfare in prevention and alleviation of suffering. This welfare can only be achieved by unity in purpose and such unity cannot come about through human means alone. It requires superhuman objectives and ability. Only the superhuman power which created man can help him realize perfection. The gradual improvement in human mentality in the past two thousand years can be expected to continue and to become worldwide providing there develops opportunity for education and freedom of communication. Education, science, and religion must be seen to exhibit their inherent unity through human communication. Fortunately this has now become possible throughout much of the world. Furthermore, energy requirements for communication are slight, in comparison with those for heavy industry or for war. Communication seems to hold the key to a way of universal peace.

Comparison of the world religions shows similarities and differences in fundamental mentality, norms of behavior and emphasis. Buddhism implies that the main events in life involve suffering and that meditation is the main antidote. Consciousness, as such, and mental training are emphasized in Buddhism. To these must be added "suffering," a result, to a large extent, of human mentality. Hinduism appears to represent, in its Avatars, stages of creative evolution of animal

11

and human life. Islam bases its teaching on the existence of "one" God and His creation. Christianity has as its central theme suffering, healing and the perfection of Christ. Spiritual and physical healing, and relief of suffering, underline the need to consider Buddhism and Christianity from similar viewpoints. They both deal with problems of stress and suffering.

A religion should be examined for new ideas, truths, ideal attitude and mentality. There is not much reward in scientific examination of a religion whose scripture is largely a rewrite of other scriptures. The term "World Religion" is taken to include all religions with a large number of adherents. The primary concern of the present investigation is with truth, concepts and principles, rather than theological theories. However, it became evident in the process of the investigation that principles of life science are clearly opposed to some scriptures. It is evident that where there is apparent contradiction this is contributed to by different languages and meanings. It is considered that individuals should read scriptures of religions other than their own so as to achieve the objective of mutual and universal understanding. Meanings of words are different when translated, and it seems that some apparent differences between Islam and Christianity can be explained on that basis and reconciled. It is necessary to have an open mentality, first of all, before undertaking a "compatibility study." The "closed mind" of a primitive, uneducated, intolerant or bigoted person is not suited to the present topic. The mentality of the reader who is biased, and already convinced that his religion is right and that others are wrong, is unscientific and unsuited to a scientific approach.

Principles which form the basis of the study of "life science and religion" can be examined only by societies which allow freedom of speech and of the written word. It is hoped that they will form a basis for religious or political change in totalitarian societies. The author appreciates the principle of human freedom, and it is this freedom which permits him to voice a scientific assessment of the areas common to religion and science. Where there is restriction of speech, publications or teaching, it is to be hoped that individuals will somehow acquire the freedom which Western society has attained.

Whereas perfection of design is evident in human creative evolution, about 4-5% of infants are born with birth defects. This fact indicates the imperfection of the human species, from a biological viewpoint. The following is from the beginning of the author's book "Birth Defects and Their Causes."

"Estimates of birth defects in hospital or general populations have varied from approximately 10 to 40 or more per 1,000. When minor degrees of abnormality are included even higher figures have been reported, especially in older children. An incidence of 5% probably represents a world average for major and minor birth defects which are present at birth, or in infancy. About half of these are major birth defects and one quarter are lethal. It is sometimes not clear to what extent minor differences in structure or function reflect physiological variability, and the borderline between normal and abnormal is not identifiable with certainty."

A further extract from the book on birth defects indicates their causes: "It is considered that 10% or less of birth defects manifest a genetic pattern. A further 10% approximately are due to chromosome aberrations; in early pregnancy the incidence of those is considerably higher than this. The remaining 80% are due to a variety of factors — these include maternal disease, drugs, infection of the uterus, placenta or foetus and insufficiency of placental blood supply." Human susceptibility to disease as well as to birth defects indicates the inadequacy of human immune mechanisms and further underlines the imperfection of man, from a biological viewpoint.

A character of God in primitive religion is omnipotence. Man was conscious, initially, of the universe, sun and planets, and his idea of God was based on creation and on physical power. The modern counterpart is biological power, and in the biology of creation of man the end product is imperfect. This evidence does not support the idea that God is all-powerful in a biological or instantaneous sense. The imperfection of human creation may be termed the "biological fall" of man;

13

the limited intelligence, self-consciousness, independence of and free will of man being the spiritual counterpart. Man's power is manifest in all branches of biological sciences and medicine, and man is a partner of God — albeit a "junior" one, especially in healing.

In every sphere of human biology there is complex development which is oriented towards specific function. This is apparent at all levels of examination. At the level of organs and tissues, cells and fibres, chromosomes and cell inclusions, the cell membrane and biological molecules, there is close relation between structure and function. This relation is the modern counterpart of man's idea of God, as a creator of the universe, in relation to physiology and design. Organization and design of biological materials are considerably more complex than that in physics; laws of astronomy and of physics were known long before human biology. There is a gradation of complexity from the atom to the human body, and particularly to the human brain. The creator designed immunity, DNA and heredity, vision, speech, hearing and the nervous system. Creation of human life and its maintenance necessitated precreative knowledge of all sciences, physical, chemical and biological.

For the preservation of life it is necessary that immune proteins be formed with structure specifically related to bacterial or viral infection. This requires design and formation of protein antibodies which change according to the infecting organism. The study of human life involves many sciences; there is no science that does not involve man and his environment. Sciences particularly related to man are anatomy or the study of structures, histology or the science of microscopy and biochemistry, which is the chemistry of biological materials. Areas of the unknown in life sciences are becoming increasingly understood daily. With progress in human biology, our ideas of God become more precise. Man's knowledge enables him to improve the condition of man and to alleviate pain and suffering. Man has thus become a partner or associate of God.

The origin of man has been the subject of considerable controversy for the past few centuries and there is still disagreement as to whether man evolved or was created instantly. From a scientific viewpoint it can be stated that there is a degree of 99% certainty about creative evolution of man. The missing link of the evolutionary chain has been claimed to have been found on many occasions and the final "proof" of evolution seems to have depended mainly on this finding. There has not been and probably will not be absolute proof, as in any biological problem. It is not generally known that science does not provide proofs; it provides probabilities. An example is the existence of an electron. What has been shown is that an electron probably existed at a particular point and time. Similarly for scientific findings in general; also for causality as a method of proof of the existence of God.

Creative evolution means development of the human species, in steps; a progressive changing of mankind along a biological system including predecessors similar to man. The main difference between these and homo sapiens was that they lacked human intelligence. A particular characteristic of prehuman primates was an evolutionary change in the brain and in the shape of the skull towards the human form. The volume of the brain increased, the connections became more complex and the cerebral cortex increased relatively to the other parts of the brain. Prehuman animals possessed mainly a palaeo or old cortex formed of the limbic system and sensory cortical areas for vision, hearing, feeling as well as motor areas for control of movement. In man, the emphasis changed to association areas of the cerebral cortex and particularly to an increase in frontal lobes. The emphasis in animals was on patterns of behavior associated with emotion. Instinctual behavior was determined by desire for food, etc. Behavior in man tended to become rational rather than instinctual or emotional. Development of the power of reason evolved with man's increased learning ability, sensitivity, memory, association, contemplation, intelligence, resulting knowledge and free will. These are facets of life which are especially well developed in

15

man. They should be given primary consideration in relating to life science and religions.

Many adopt attitudes about evolution, without having the knowledge necessary to form a qualified opinion. In discussions, one frequently hears opinions by persons who never studied evolution or who are prejudiced by limited knowledge. In science, it is realized that disagreements are not personal; in religions, arguments often become personal since they are frequently between "laymen" or non-specialists. Theologians have tended, especially in the past, to confine themselves to one religion, in reading, attitude and belief. Ignorance of other religions tends to perpetuate differences of opinion and to promote prejudice. Disagreements are based on ignorance. A selection of evidence concerning evolution would be out of place here, since it would be limited and therefore biased. The question is left open, so that a reader may study biological sciences and form his own opinion. What is clear is that there is gradation or stepwise increase in complexity among species and sub-species. This is evident at the Darwinian level of gross anatomy. It is clear also in the physiology of the heart, lungs, kidneys, brain and every system of the body. This gradation is evident in a variety of life sciences, including biochemistry on a comparatives basis.

The elegance in design in biology of body systems, organs, tissues, cells, fibers and fluids becomes clear on study of biological subjects. It supports the presence of purposefulness in creation. It carries to the microscopic and molecular level our understanding of organization in life science. There are in creation, however, limitations and imperfections. Birth defects are present in man and other species; associated personal and family suffering is a reality. Many diseases remain to be overcome, and man's ability to study himself, in life science, confers on him the power to partner God, at a medical level.

The delegation of power by God, to man, was intended for the benefit of man. Such good can only come through increased knowledge and understanding among different races

16

and religions, followed by suitable action for the promotion of human welfare. Medicine provides prevention or cure of disease, where possible. Improvement of human welfare requires cooperation of religions and life science. An attitude of learning, understanding, and loving is essential for prevention of suffering, for healing, for psychological and spiritual improvement of man and even for human survival.

CHAPTER 2

CONSCIOUSNESS, STRESS AND REVELATION

Human consciousness is best considered first of all in comparison with consciousness in non-human primates and other animals. Animals can see, hear and are conscious but they are not aware of themselves as distinct beings separate in their consciousness from the rest of creation. We believe that animals are not, therefore, self-conscious, that they do not think of themselves in the same way as man does. Man developed intelligence and knowledge and he became aware that he existed as a separate being, independent of God in will and capable of acquiring knowledge and deciding on behavior. Man became aware of his own emotions and developed a rationality, a sense of self-analysis depending on his mental detachment, in that he could consider himself objectively. He became self-conscious. Elsewhere in nature animals are the subjects and related to their environment, which is objective and formed of objects. In man, subject and object may be one. Man's thought extends not only throughout the field of human knowledge but also to himself, even to his own mind and thoughts. This one-

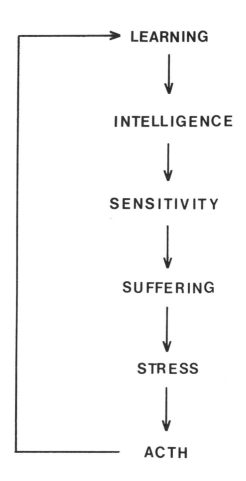

Figure 1

Proposed cycle concerning human development of intelligence, sensitivity and associated susceptibility to stress. The latter produces increased secretion of ACTH. This hormone has been shown, in laboratory animals, to enhance learning.

ness of subject and object is unique in man and human consciousness is quite different from that of animals. Man has developed also, to a much greater extent, the mental attributes of emotions and reason.

Animals' behavior is determined in instincts and by desires which promote the survival of the individual and of the species. Such instincts involve eating, drinking, reproduction, sleeping, etc. Animal patterns of activity are largely predetermined or predestined by their anatomical, physiological and psychological mental structure, determined by creative evolution. Animals do not possess free will similar to that in man. The higher functions of the mind of man are not achieved by animals. They do not possess the learning ability, the knowledge or understanding, or the thinking mechanism of the human mind. Also animals' ability to communicate is far more limited than that of man.

The consciousness of man is located in the brain — precise localization is not possible. However, electrical stimulation of different areas of the cerebral cortex has brought back memories, in patients, of previous experiences. Electrical stimulation during operations under local anesthesia resulted in the patients remembering previous events clearly, including visual aspects, music and associated emotions. Storage of memorized events is a function of the cerebral cortex and of the association area between the visual, auditory, sensory and speech centers (Wernicke's area) and others. Physiological evidence supports the view that events which are experienced become memorized in a pattern of physico-chemical change. This pattern is both electrical and chemical: the electrical aspect is a three-dimensional pattern of changes. Biochemical changes involve proteins and nucleoproteins. Some proteins have been isolated which are involved in long and in short term memory. The transmission of excitation between nerve cells is now well understood, physically and chemically, and recognized as due to neurotransmitters. These are chemical substances, and include adrenaline, dopamine and noradrenaline. Polypeptides, endorphins and enkephalins act as opiates and prevent or diminish the sense of pain. Apparently psychological factors alter their secretion, as well as that of stress hormones, which also enhance pain sensation.

The reticular activating system (RAS) or reticular formation (RF) is a network of neurones in the midbrain which has connections, direct or indirect, with every part of the nervous system. This system regulates the level of sensitivity of the brain and also selective concentration. Thus, the reticular system is mainly responsible for the level of consciousness or sleep and it also selectively concentrates mental processes. The reticular formation is the central co-ordinating subcortical system of the brain. It correlates information and puts it in storage in the cerebral cortex. It is in contact, physiologically, with previous experiences, and computer-like, selects, regulates, associates and concentrates. The reticular activating system is the main controller of the level of consciousness and its content. The RAS is the supervisor and regulator of mental processes and is the modern counterpart of the seat of the mind or of the soul. The reticular system is involved in different phases of meditation, as well as one pointed concentration which is part of the meditative process. In this context the reticular activating system transcends the other parts of the human brain. It controls sensation; it coordinates impressions with memory; it selects areas for consideration. The RAS is involved in processes of mental training as well as in psychology and psychiatry. This system is closely involved in concentration, meditation, contemplative processes and mysticism.

The contribution of the reticular formation, to alertness and concentration, is determined in part by control of secretion of noradrenaline and other neurotransmitters. At the anterior end of the reticular formation lies the center for the sympathetic autonomic system and this secretes noradrenaline and other catecholamines and thus helps to regulate levels of human sensitivity. The process of learning, the differences in sensitivity and excitability, and the impressions, associations and memories of the human mind are affected considerably by the reticular activating system and neurotransmitters. The differences in sensitivity in individuals and in different species appears to have a genetic component and to be related to intelligence, emotional reaction and patterns of behavior.

Cosmic consciousness is a state of mind where one's awareness is psychically united with the cosmos or entire universe. This unity has a material basis in Buddhism which emphasizes the unity of all things, biological, mental and material. The oneness, based on a unity and interdependence of these, is so stressed, in Buddhism, that one is said to be dependent, for existence or being, on the other. Human mental processes are considered to depend on their environment and are said not to exist or to be capable of existing without the objects of thought. One of the main aspects of cosmic consciousness is the deletion of individual consciouness. Becoming "one with the cosmos" means that the individual loses his self-consciousness and becomes "not conscious" in Buddhist meditation. Similarly, nirvana is a state free of mental disturbances and even of normal mental function; there is no physiological reason to consider that it is supernatural. In simple terms it is similar to animal consciousness whereby an animal is not aware of his separateness of existence. Christianity emphasizes individual conscious in life and after death.

Stress

Human stress, illness, anxiety and suffering are important themes of medical science and religion. Literally the word stress means strain, extension, bending or application of tension. Its meaning is physical and psychological. Physical causes are heat, cold, pressure changes, movement, excessive sound or light, and pain. Physical stress includes injury, suffering and disease. Psychological stress involves excessive mental anxiety. Man is partly responsible for human stress: human knowledge leading to self-consciouness, selfishness and lack of consideration of one's neighbor are the basis for much of mental stress. Buddha said that much of life is suffering; being born or giving birth, being ill, desiring or craving, aging and dying. Much of Buddhism is a philosophy of stress rather than

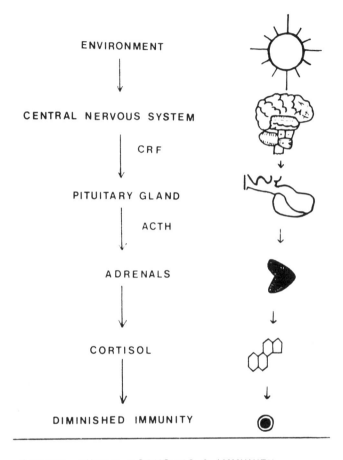

ENVIRONMENT

CENTRAL NERVOUS SYSTEM

CRF

PITUITARY GLAND

ACTH

ADRENALS

CORTISOL

DIMINISHED IMMUNITY

STRESS, HUMAN HORMONES & IMMUNITY

Figure 2

The axis of stress. This involves the external and internal environment, in physical, chemical or biological changes. The response is mediated through the brain and pituitary-adrenal axis, increasing secretion of the stress hormones ACTH and cortisol. Administration of a large dose of either of these hormones diminishes immunity.

a religion; causes of suffering are given and ways of avoiding suffering described. Practice of meditation is prescribed to clear the mind of psychological anxiety and of sensitivity to physical pain. This contrasts with Christianity, in which loving (mankind) underlines the prevention and treatment of physical suffering.

Life science, medicine, Buddhism and Christianity have a common basis, involving human mental development. They involve philosophies of life based on intelligence and rationality. Hinduism is based on the undesirability of human materialist motivation. Attachment to worldly things and desires are said to underline man's "imperfection" and involve distraction, disorientation or turning away from God to material things. The basic theme is similar to original "sin." The meaning and content of original "sin" are thus shared by these three religions — simply that man has developed limited knowledge and materialism. A recommendation to take our minds off "worldly attachments" is common to all three. Islam, however, deals with a way of life as well as religion and does not include "original sin" or prescribe detachment from material things.

Human suffering is dependent primarily on human sensitivity and intelligence. Emotions are linked, in mankind, with knowledge. Our ability for greater emotion (than in other species) determines a risk of a sense of loss. Love carries with it the hazard of suffering through loss, and attachment to material things involves detachment. The more we love things or persons the greater we suffer when the relationship ceases. Development of human consciousness exposes us to greater sensitivity to personal loss. Human learning, memory, understanding, and emotion all lead to independent thought and decision. Human independence (of God and of purely instinctual behavior) and free will lead to increased responsibility, a sense of aloneness, or separation from God, a tendency to dependence on others, and to suffering or stress, to which man is especially susceptible.

Stress involves the nervous system and hormones. Stress hormones can be measured and their levels give indications of de-

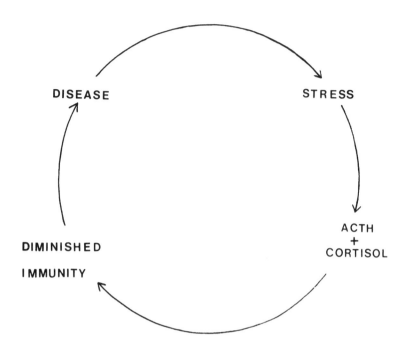

CYCLE RELATING TO STRESS AND

DISEASE IN MAN

Figure 3

Proposed cycle relating stress to diminished immunity. This is based, to some extent, on the stress axis shown in Figure 2 and the increased levels of ACTH, which we found in diseases. Disease is considered to increase stress, and stress to enhance disease, thus forming a vicious circle. The diminished immunity in human pregnancy to some infections may be due to effects of stress.

grees of stress or suffering. Chemicals are produced in the brain and in glands in normal actions and reactions. Some of these increase in the blood in response to stress. Two of particular interest are cortisol (from the adrenal glands) and ACTH (adrenocorticotropic hormone: formed by the pituitary gland). Others, known as catecholamines, are adrenaline, noradrenaline, and dopamine. Many chemical transmitters are produced by brain cells and changes in blood levels of these result from exposure to stress.

Measures of stress, most commonly examined at present, are ACTH and cortisol. In our laboratory we measured these in pregnancy, prior to labor; in patients with diseases of the various systems of the body (nervous, digestive, respiratory etc.), with infections or with tumors. We measured ACTH and cortisol levels in blood plasma in late pregnancy and examined the relation between these and subsequent duration of labor in 40 women. We found a direct relation between blood levels of ACTH and of cortisol and the duration of labor, using computer analysis. Higher levels of stress hormones were associated with longer (subsequent) labor. This is evidence that human congenital stress is due mainly to psychological strain. Such stress followed man's development of intelligence, knowledge, and free will, with associated liability to suffering.

A cycle has been proposed by the author relating stress to pituitary and adrenal activity, to explain the profound (up to thousandfold) increase in urinary output of oestriol during human pregnancy. This cycle includes stress acting through the brain and endocrine glands and also a stimulating effect of oestrogens on the pituitary-adrenal axis. Oestriol is an end-product of oestrogen metabolism and its very high output is unique in the human species. Since it is similar in structure to other oestrogens and an end-product of their metabolism, it can be expected to inhibit contractions of the uterus and lead to longer labor (congenital distress) of the human subject than in non-human primates or other species.

Blood levels of the stress hormone ACTH were found in our laboratory to be elevated in tumors, infections, diseases of the central nervous, cardiovascular, respiratory and other systems.

Cortisol was increased in diseases of the reproductive system, circulation, blood, and in patients suffering from tumor. It is proposed that severe stress may trigger a cycle whereby disease and stress interact to lead to diminished immunity, thus promoting disease. Disease is considered to act as a stress, causing increase in ACTH and (in some systematic disease) in cortisol. High levels of these hormones are known to diminish immunity and thus lead to increase in disease. ACTH is considerably increased in man, for short periods, due to spurts in secretion and this may lead to further risk of diminishing resistance to disease.

The meaning of suffering is feeling pain or worrying, being patient, desiring, being under a strain, tolerating unpleasantness, sustaining a personal or family loss, receiving punishment, being isolated, lacking something one has become used to, grieving, feeling sad, feeling unwell, being under a physical or mental strain. Many more meanings could be given for this human feeling of sadness, or inadequacy. It implies mental discontent, a natural anxiety, an inborn unhappiness and yearning for happiness. Love causes suffering, through desire, separation or loss. Hate causes suffering, since it makes one "feel ill" towards another. The medical approach is by rationality, and life science, by working on suffering — finding out its causes, preventing it and curing it. The policy of medicine of lessening pain should be pursued by all mankind in working towards a society free of suffering. Incidentally, this is the same as the Christian mentality and objective, apparently alone, among religions, in its foundation, principles, mentality and objectives.

Revelation and Reason

Revelation is a special feature of scriptures, which can be judged for truth content by compatibility with life science. Religion has depended to a great extent on "revelation" of knowledge or "fact" to individuals. This applies to life science also. In life science, however, information can be confirmed and results and "facts" can be investigated for their factuality.

Science is open to all, individually and especially collectively, to obtain knowledge of God's creation. Religion is now being approached in the same way, with the same attitude, scientifically, with an open mind, almost agnostically; with a mentality which is willing to accept change, to accept the possibility of truth in one or all religions; not with a closed, biased, primitive mind. Education in life science leads us all to respect "our neighbor" and to acquire empathy which is an insight into "his" point of view, taking into consideration his personality and environment. Man exhibits many variations in mentality, language, culture and religion. Similarly life science has many component subjects, e.g. biochemistry, anatomy, physiology, medicine etc.

We require many years of training before we are able to understand medicine. Similarly, primitive concepts of God gradually replaced beliefs that Thunder or the sun was God, by an understanding that "God" is a scientist with universal knowledge, a mathematician with infinite understanding, a life scientist constantly creatively evolving human immune mechanisms, as well as the consciousness and mentality of man. This mentality includes attitude to work and creativity, responsibility to mankind and to God's design for life, especially human life.

Evidence from biological and medical research is fundamental in our beliefs on creation, evolution, healing, imperfection of man and human susceptibility to disease. Reason, observations and experiments are the basis of science, which is knowledge obtained by human methods. Revelation is knowledge revealed by God, directly or through divine "messengers." Since there are many scriptures which are claimed to have been revealed by God to man, it is reasonable to examine them for content of truth by scientific method. The basis for scientific assessment is that a number of people confirm an observation. Life science is, by nature, skeptical of revelation claimed by a single individual, and this is considered "private revelation."

Creation and maintenance of human life are considered the most complex acts of God. His revelations should preferably be accompanied by an action which involves similar biological complexity, such as instantaneous healing. Biological events, especially healing, are more the province of life science than physical occurrences, and obviously especially relevant as evidence for divine revelation. Traditionally, revelation has been the origin of knowledge of God, of creation, of standards for behavior and (in some religions) of laws. The modern counterpart of revelation is reason, and this has been used in life science to provide understanding of creative evolution, of design, human biology, suffering, disease and healing. Reason, medical knowledge, and understanding lead to compassion, healing and alleviation of suffering. Those who become involved in life science including medicine develop a mentality of "neighborly love" which is Christian. Revelation concerning development of man is found in Genesis. It has now become possible to investigate Genesis (meaning the development of man) and its consequences, congenital stress in women, as foretold to Eve. The section of Genesis concerning the "Fall" or imperfection of man is central to life science, evolution and comparative religions. In the latter, the development of human intelligence, knowledge and free will, form the core, as "original sin," of the basis for Christian doctrines. Fundamentally, the "Fall" means that man developed as a finite being and original sin means "free will."

Our knowledge of God is through science and the scriptures; our "proofs" of God's existence are scientific. The most important contents of Genesis concern "creation" of early man. The Koran describes God as "Creator" and cites evidence from nature for "his" existence. The "proofs" for the existence of God are like scientific "facts" and are not absolute. The evidence is circumstantial; the certainty is less than 100%. Change in human concepts, and in understanding of God and of religion, is inevitable in view of advances in all branches of science.

The existence of God became "revealed" to a primitive people by perception of the sky, stars, moon, sun, agriculture, i.e. scientific observation. For modern man knowledge of God is through life science, human creative evolution, consciousness, reason, understanding, chromosomal, genetic and biochemical knowledge. Life science leads to a "universal understanding" and this leads from self-consciousness to knowledge of others and thus to compassion. This compassion depends on understanding the other person's thinking, feeling, attitude, suffering and behavior. When we "put ourselves" in the position of another, mentally, we can "see" why he behaves in a certain way, believing in different "religion" or in apparent enmity to us. God is capable of supernatural acts and when He "revealed himself" in some way to man He used light, speech and healing. It is stated in the Bhagavad Gita and John's Gospel that the spirit of God or Counsellor "descends" to inspire man with guidance in the proper path at certain times of crisis in man's existence. Revelation of truth of knowledge has come to religious, layman, and scientist alike. Only among scientists can the "revelation" be put to the test of scientific investigation and considered open to scientific evaluation.

Where revelation has included the hearing of a voice (or voices) by an individual, then it is especially desirable from a scientific viewpoint that supporting evidence be available, such as signs or miracles. There has been evidence of supernatural happenings, at Lourdes and Fatima, including miracles. These have also added evidence for the visions of Our Lord's Mother in Cairo, though this seemed unnecessary since thousands of people saw the apparitions of Mary. "Revealed" material loses credibility if it is not compatible with life science. In mystic meditation, revelation of knowledge of God is frequently expected, but reports of individual experiences have varied considerably from person to person, and no scientific value can be attached to experience or emotions described.

An orderliness, sequence and rationality should apply to revelation if it is to be accepted by the general public, especially educated people. There should be consistency, as in scientific experiments, and, obviously God should not contradict Himself or "change His mind." God should not be "sectarian," in being well disposed to one race or people. Such an attitude is not acceptable to science, which considers it to be attributed to God by man. God should not confine His communications to one language, nor end them, as if man had become sufficiently mature and rational (which he clearly is not), to be left alone without God. In scientific learning we build upon previous knowledge and we become inspired by new ideas. In religion, the same principle applies — learning by experience. There is no stage at which all religious knowledge has been reached. Since both Religion and Science are about creation they complement one another. To say that man acquired all necessary knowledge in either, at any time, puts him on a level with God in his knowledge. It is obvious that man will be learning during all his existence. Scientists have the humility to believe this; it is the ignorant who do not realize the limitations of their knowledge. Increase in knowledge of religion and of science are necessary for implementation of the destinies and purposes of man.

Our scientific and religious learning is limited, like walking, to one step at a time, each one following the one before. We come to know more about God when we learn more about the most complex of sciences, i.e. life science. And the knowledge of life science helps us understand the principles of human development and the social and medical implications of religious "commandments" or "regulations." Where it is clear that a commandment should apply, in the interests of human health and survival, then such a commandment or regulation will be or should be advocated by life science, as well as by religion. Where a local, national or village rule does not necessarily need to apply to all of mankind, then it is not in the interests of all that such a rule is forced on them. Nor should local principles of violence and retaliation be promoted, or allowable, in the interests of "future happiness and peace."

Education leads to maturity and wisdom and spread of education can lead to universal understanding of the principles which relate to life science. Education should not be confined or sectarian, or excessively nationalist-political. All mankind is created by God and no one group of people has all knowledge or the "final word" of God. A multiplicity of views is better than one and furthers understanding of religion. The modern decrease in religious belief is, in part, due to narrow and specialist education. A broad education in life science and religion increases understanding of the creation of man, principles concerning his survival, the purpose of his rationality, the importance of human life and the imperfection which characterizes man, physically, mentally and spiritually. Rationality, science and material welfare are increasing and cooperation of rational with emotional aspects of human development is greater than ever. Human emotions are older, and more primitive than reason in human development.

The word "Nirvana" includes reason and all knowledge, a prerequisite to a state of universal understanding of peace which is the objective of civilization. It corresponds to the "Kingdom of heaven" which means spirituality and perfection, on earth as well as in heaven, to be experienced through learning, understanding, knowledge and love. In private revelation there is always the problem of how much is from the person's own mind, and how much is from God or spirit (good or evil). No individual can be proved scientifically to have experienced revelation from God. It is reasonable to expect that God generally reveals an important message to numbers of persons. There are many examples in the gospels and in apparitions (see final chapter). Revealed material, which is inspired, is affected and sometimes modified by the mind of the individual involved. Thus, for example, there are some parts of the Old Testament which show the influence of the writer. This is not to say that the main message of these is false. In fact, historical accounts support the main happenings in religious scriptures. They do show, however, that scriptures are partly historical, at least and that they are not, as once thought, completely revealed. It has been claimed, for scriptures, that each was the word of God and the reiteration of this claim is no proof of its authenticity. To what extent revelation to an individual is affected by consciousness is impossible to determine. In a scientific age one can reasonably use a logical and scientific approach as a parameter for measurement of authenticity. The deletion of stanzas and substitution of new ones, changes in religious precepts, the deliberate seeking after mystical states and experiences — all these are indicative of a human element. In the long-term future, clearly accurate accounts such as Mark's gospel will be recognized not so much for their revelation, but for their historical reports of events.

CHAPTER 3

CONFUCIANISM AND TAOISM

Confucianism

The fundamental concept of Confucianism has been summarized as follows: "If there be righteousness in the heart, there will be beauty in the character. If there be beauty in the character there will be harmony in the home. If there be harmony in the home, there will be order in the nation. If there be order in the nation, there will be peace in the world." This central theme is more about ethics than religion, attitude than legality, love of others rather than selfishness, self in relation to society rather than ritual praying or pilgrimage. The advice of Jesus, "Love your neighbor as yourselves," is an even shorter summary of the ideal way of life — and religion — of man. It has been said that the Chinese did not embrace Christianity — nor did Buddhists, elsewhere — because they already had inherited its basic philosophy. "Do unto others as you would they do unto you," said Christ; Confucius' version, "What you do not wish done to yourself, do not do to others," may be negative, but is similar, in principle.

Kung Fu-tzu or Kung the Master has been known as the First

Teacher, in China, for over two thousand years. No innovator, Confucius summarized and taught Chinese tradition about how people are to live with one another. His philosophy had developed as an inherent pattern of living in the Chinese people. Confucius integrated ancient Chinese traditions of attitude and behavior. He is credited with popularizing Chinese proverbs, which could be the basic philosophy at family, community, national and international levels. The universal peace which could result from practice of Confucius' ideals is mirrored by the universal mental and physical peace, foreseen in almost all world religions, in the future of man. Politics uses other means, however, for attaining materialist ends and must be credited with a major share in the causation of human suffering. In this respect politics is opposed to religion and to ultimate universal human peace, being human, nationalist, separatist, materialist, selfish and divisive.

Confucius was born about the same time as Buddha, in Shantung province around 551 B.C., according to Western calculation. His father died when he was young — his family was poor — but he became interested in learning at an early age. He became a tutor, though spending some time in the "civil service" of the Government. He "specialized" in human behavior and ethics, in philosophy, and in the relation between individuals and between man and society.

There are five main concepts which outline and summarize Confucius' principles of human mentality and attitude. These are:

1) Jen: the relation between individuals,
2) Chun-tzu: gentleness and consideration,
3) Li: manner and methods,
4) Te: power for good,
5) Wen: the arts: culture.

(1) Jen: this means benevolence or love and involves particularly the emotional relation between individuals. It includes one's mentality and attitude towards others. It implies a change from self-oriented to "other"-oriented feeling. There is a close relationship between Jen and the extroversion or love of

36

neighbor attitude advocated by Christ. An implication also underlines this tradition, of introversion as an undesirable quality of the human mind, insofar as it leads to selfishness. At the center of Jen is a respect for human life; this leads to self-respect and respect for others. Some primitive societies do not have this quality and their lack of it is reflected in their way of life, tradition and religion. One thinks of desert tribes, where the survival instinct dictates reciprocity in killing, and barbarian, brutal punishments for crime. Confucius stated he never witnessed perfect Jen. "The determined scholar and the man of Jen will even sacrifice their lives to preserve their Jen complete." Clearly the unique example of perfection in Jen is Jesus Christ, in his philosophy, doing good, and self-sacrifice.

(2) Chun-tzu: This is the manner or quality of relation between persons. It reflects ones mentality and attitude. It refers to mode of behavior, speech and action towards another person. It bespeaks the underlying emotion of Jen, though it may be merely "outward show," which should not be mistaken for sincerity itself. The person with Chun-tzu is genuinely interested in society. He is usually cultured, broadly educated, considerate, compassionate and interested in social welfare. In this modern world such a person takes an active part in social work, so as to help other people to a reasonable and happy standard of life. Some politicians — probably the minority — have this quality. In general, few people could be said to exhibit a genuine Chun-tzu.

(3) Li: The proper way — tradition — grace and correctness in personal and social activities. Language and the proper use of words and names are emphasized in Li. Tradition and upbringing, family training and education — these are the main influences on one's manner of behavior. An excessive materialism — when this is a sympton of selfishness — runs counter to Li. Social graces are not necessarily related to income; in fact, if a relation exists it may be inverse. We often find that the poor are better mannered, more neighborly and compassionate. Their social position has burdened them with an excess of suffering. They learn forbearance and understanding. The rich, on the other hand, are inherently selfish

and lack the "enriching experiences" and excellent qualities of (many of) their poor fellowmen.

Moderation and the avoidance of excesses, the "mean" or middle way, was advocated in all human behavior by Confucius. This is in contrast with the extremes and fanaticism of some individuals, nations, and "religions." Reasonableness was always desirable, in human behavior. The urgent need for self-control at individual, communal, national, and international levels is much in evidence today with the availability of lethal power. Clearly, human sense of responsibility has not developed as quickly as physical sciences. Perhaps this can be expected, as a general principle. The greater complexity of human understanding leads to a slowness in learning from experience. Suffering is a great teacher, but memories are short; humanity has often had to re-learn by bitter experience. The cure for suffering is in education, to a level of appreciation of life — particularly of human life.

Li incorporates relations within the family, between friends and between ruler and subject. Confucius recognized the family unit as a pillar of society and family ties are highly valued in rural China. Parental control and guidance as well as respect for parents, duties of children, including obedience; these, as well as respect for the aged, all form a pattern that emphasizes the importance of the "extended family" in Chinese tradition.

Li also means ritual. The pattern of behavior, of action towards others, of social and political ceremonies as determined by tradition, is included in Li. Such tradition determines a moderating influence and sets patterns rather than laws for governing people's activities.

(4) Te: Power-Rule-Government-Control: The philosophy of ruling is related closely to the example of the ruler(s), according to Confucius. Example leads to imitation and a chain reaction. Breaking family and other ties leads to discontinuity and loss of tradition. Totalitarian rule was opposed by Confucius as leading to discontent, inefficiency and loss of motivation. Example and mentality are more important in Confucianism than oppressive rule. Confucius is quoted as saying, "Oppressive rule is more cruel than a tiger." Quotations from

Confucius on Te include: "The north polar star keeps its place and all the stars turn towards it." "To govern is to keep straight; if you lead the people straight, which of your subjects will venture to fall out of line?" "What need is there of death penalty in government? If you showed a sincere desire to be good, your people would likewise be good. The virtue of the prince is like unto wind; that of the people like unto grass. For it is the nature of grass to bend when the wind blows upon it."

(5) Wen: This means culture, and includes literature, art, music, etc. "the arts of peace." Culture, Confucius said, reflected a society's mental development, and is more powerful than war in determining international spread of an ideology or mentality. The impact of literature is important — prose and poetry are probably greatest among the humanities. Education and communication are largely based on literature and the faculties of Arts place considerable emphasis on languages. Cultures and traditions are given far less attention in modern media than they might have been about 500 B.C. There is a neglect of religion in modern media which reflects the materialism of Western society. A return to the Confucian emphasis on culture and tradition in international relations is advisable, in the near future, to promote international understanding not merely at a specialist level, but at the level of basic education.

The borderline, if such exists, between Confucianism and Religion, is indistinct. There appears to have been a belief in God as the "Mother of Nature" and in the principles of heaven and hell and a "life after death." In ancient China there were sacrifices by the village leader, the "Son of Heaven"; a practice still extant is referral by a variety of means to heavenly and ancestral spirits for guidance.

Taoism

The Tao Te Ching ("The Way and its Power") is a summary of early Chinese teaching, whose author is said to be Lao Tzu ("Old Master"). Born about 604 B.C., he was considered by Confucius to have been a man of outstanding ability and benevolence. Tao means "The Absolute," "Supernatural," "God," "Ultimate Reality," "Creator." "The Transcendent Being" which is beyond human understanding and description, is a universal spirit which designs, guides, controls, and is immanent in all things. The Way implies the "path or Way," designed by God for man, which is God's Will for human mentality and behavior.

Undertstanding or description of the "Supreme Reality" is said not to be possible for mankind, nor can the "Supreme Being" be completely known or described in human words or terms. The concept is of transcendent, absolute, infinite, eternal being — the perfect and unchanging. This corresponds to Hindu and Christian belief — there is not the emphasis, or even proposal of, a single, "one" God, found in Judaism and Islam, in pure monotheistic form. As in Hinduism (particularly) human experience of the Supreme Eternal Being is by meditation, rather than contemplation. The Tao, however, is understood also in relation to design, creation and beauty of nature and "God" is known through His manifestations in the created universe, in plants, animals, man and in the guiding and controlling power in all things. This corresponds to the Western concept originating in Genesis. In contrast to Christianity, which refers to God as "Father," Taoism describes nature as the "Mother of the World." Closer, in fact, is the Christian "Universal Spirit," which indicates the "Unknown," or Supernatural force which permeates all things, including the human mind, which the spirit seeks to guide in "the right way" (of life). The Tao, relating as it does to the Spirit, admonishes the "putting aside of the Self" and clearing of the mind of earthly senses and desires, so as to fulfill mental tranquillity, mystic meditation. All selfishness and self-seeking caused by human desires should be cast aside in the quest for spirituality — in this fundamental concept, Taoism shares the "original sin" of Christianity and the "attachment" so frowned on in the Bhagavad Gita. In Islam there is a contrasting absence of such a concept, as in Judaism. Both of these religions may be said to be materialist in the absence of such an important underlying principle. They have been claimed to be political systems rather than spiritual foundations. Christ's plea to "Give to Caesar the things that are Caesar's" exhibits a fundamental spirituality, and underlines the commom basis of spirituality in Christianity, Taoism and Hinduism. From this point of view Taoism recognized the self-seeking desires of man and their foundation on human self-consciousness. The material aspects of life were considered to be detrimental to the "inner self" or soul, and a form of meditation was advocated in which the mind was stripped of sensuality and of desires, resulting in a deeper consciousness of the Absolute, as in Hinduism. The state of meditation was known to promote selflessness and tranquillity, and to curb desires and selfishness. The central theme of this aspect of meditation is similar to the spirituality of the meditative process in Christianity and Hinduism; Buddhism also, if we consider its theological or religious aspects.

Confucius is believed to have visited Lao Tzu and to have been highly impressed by his discussions with him, of philosophy and religion. He described him as a dragon in his mentality, transcending wind and clouds and reaching heavenly heights in his genius. The author, it is said, of the Tao Te Ching (literally, the Way and the Power) is believed to have written the Tao near the Hankao Pass, in west China, on his way to Tibet. The Tao Te Ching is a short "book," of about 5,000 Chinese characters. Its survival, to this day, is testimony to the quality of its content — and of its uniqueness.

Tao means the way in physical, spiritual and psychological terms. It relates to the universe, the spiritual "mother of nature" and also to the way of ideal behavior — the Way of life. In general content and principles, in its general meaning, and its three dimensions — spiritual, universal (creative) and behavioral — the "Way and the Power" resembles other religions, being closest perhaps to Hinduism and Christianity. It lacks, however, the Christian approach to suffering (i.e. prevention of suffering and healing).

The spiritual dimension of Tao Te Ching found expression in practices of contemplation and meditation. A mentality of mystic oneness with the absolute was aimed at through detachment from sensuality and materialism. A state of psychic and spiritual being was aimed at; an altered consciousness, a state akin to the nirvana of Buddhism, or the oneness with the absolute of Hindu aspirations. Accompanying Yogic practices, involving breathing exercises, helped to unite physical, psychological and psychic in a union of perfection and cosmic consciousness. Mystic practices, however, tended to be followed by only a few from each communal group; their spiritual influence, however, was (and is) considered to benefit all in the spread of benevolent attitude.

Ch. 1.
1. "The Tao that can be trodden is not the enduring and unchanging Tao."

2. "(Conceived of as) having no name, it is the Originator of heaven and earth; (conceived of as) having a name, it is the Mother of all things."

3. "Always without desire we must be found,
If its deep mastery we would sound;
But if desire always within us be
Its outer fringe is all that we shall see."

4. "Under these two aspects, it is really the same; but as development takes place, it receives the different names. Together we call them the Mystery. Where the Mystery is the deepest is the gate of all that is subtle and wonderful."

The concept of transcendence and unknowable nature of the eternal being is apparent here, as well as that of Creator and "Mother," in contrast to the term "Father" in Christianity.

Humility is a virtue of Christianity. "He who exalteth himself, shall be humbled." "The last shall be first." Materialism is opposed to spirituality and leads to gratification of desires and selfishness, which is the "attachment" of the Gita and the basis for competitiveness in social relations. This selfishness has characterized politics and led to human conflict and aggression.

Ch. 22.
1. "The partial becomes complete, the crooked, straight; the empty full, the

worn out, new. He whose (desires) are few gets them; he whose (desires) are many goes astray."

2. "Therefore the sage holds in his embrace the one thing (of humility) and manifests it to all the world. He is free from self- display, and therefore he shines; from self-assertion, and therefore he is distinguished; from self-boasting, and therefore his merit is acknowledged; from self-complacency, and therefore he acquires superiority. It is because he is thus free from striving that therefore no one in the world is able to strive with him."

The same sentiment is echoed here, underlying the "self" and self consciousness as a cause of human problems.

Ch. 24.   "He who stands on his tiptoes does not stand firm; he who stretches his legs does not walk (easily). (So), he who displays himself does not shine; he who asserts his own views is not distinguished; he who vaunts himself does not find his merit acknowledged; he who is self- conceited has no superiority allowed to him. Such conditions, viewed from the standpoint of the Tao, are like remnants of food, or a tumor on the body, which all dislike. Hence those who pursue (the course) of the Tao do not adopt and allow them."

The concept of changelessness is shared with other religions. In the Koran, however, God is considered to change verses and substitute new ones for those omitted.

Ch.25.   1. "There was something undefined and complete, coming into existence before Heaven and Earth. How still it was and formless, standing alone, and undergoing no change, reaching everywhere and in

43

no danger (of being exhausted). It may be regarded as the Mother of all things."

2. "I do not know its name, and I give it the designation of the Tao (the Way or Course). Making an effort (further) to give it a name I call it The Great."

Ch. 30.   1. "He who would assist a lord of men in harmony with the Tao will not assert his mastery in the kingdom by force of arms. Such a course is sure to meet with its proper return."

Ch. 31.   1. "Now arms, however beautiful, are instruments of evil omen, hateful, it may be said, to all creatures. Therefore they who have the Tao do not like to employ them."

2. "The superior man ordinarily considers the left hand the most honorable place, but in time of war the right hand. Those sharp weapons are instruments of evil omen, and not the instruments of the superior man; he uses them only on the compulsion of necessity. Calm and repose are what he prizes; victory (by force or arms) is to him undesirable. To consider this desirable would be to delight in the slaughter of men; and he who delights in the slaughter of men cannot get his will in the kingdom."

The sentiment of this verse is echoed in Christianity. It is counter to materialism and agrees with spiritual motives of tranquillity and selflessness.

Ch. 46.   2. "There is no guilt greater than to sanction ambition; no calamity greater than to be discontented with one's lot; no fault greater then the wish to be getting. Therefore the sufficiency of contentment

is an enduring and unchanging sufficiency."

Increase in learning is a basic principle in science, and is common to all cultures in modern society. It should extend beyond community, racial and national boundaries if knowledge is to lead to universal understanding and to peace.

Ch. 48.	1. "He who devotes himself to learning (seeks) from day to day to increase (his knowledge); he who devotes to the Tao (seeks) from day to day to diminish (his doing)."
Ch. 49.	2. "To those who are good (to me), I am good; and to those who are not good (to me), I am also good; and thus (all) get to be good. To those who are sincere (with me), I am sincere; and to those who are not sincere (with me), I am also sincere, and thus (all) get to be sincere."

This philosophy is the ideal and is the same as the Christian principle. It contrasts with Islam which retains the primitive "eye for an eye" of the old Christian scripture. The philosophy of Christ seeks to abolish this as well as primitive punishment, e.g. stoning, scourging and severance of limbs, for breaking the laws.

The absence of divine control over man is accepted by cultures, apart from Islam, and Moslems are, by definition, obedient to God. In recent times, however, the concept of free will, which is the basis of Christianity, is being incorporated by some into Islam. This is difficult to reconcile with predestination, which seems to be taught in the Koran.

Ch. 51.	3. "Thus it is that the Tao produces (all things), nourishes them, brings them to their full growth, nurses them, completes them, matures them, maintains them, and overspreads them."
	4. "It produces them and makes no claim to the possession of them; it carries them

45

through their process and does not vault in its ability in doing so; it brings them to maturity and exercises no control over them; this is called its mysterious operation."

The concept of children of the creator guarding virtue and following the "Way" of the creator has much in common with principles taught by Christ.

Ch. 52.   1. "(The Tao) which originated all under the sky is to be considered as the mother of them all."

2. "When the mother is found, we know what her children should be. When one knows that he is his mother's child, and proceeds to guard (the qualities of) the mother that belong to him, to the end of his life he will be free from all peril."

One is reminded in the following verses of the attitude of Christ to similar people, especially the rich, who were advised to give up their wealth and follow his teaching of perfection in all-giving and in spirituality. Islam, in contrast, deals with material things and encourages man to enjoy them.

Ch. 53.   1. "If I were suddenly to become known and (put into a position to) conduct (a government) according to the Great Tao, what I should be most afraid of would be a boastful display."

2. "The great Tao (or way) is very level and easy; but people love the by-ways."

3. "Their court (yards and buildings) shall be kept, but their fields shall be ill-cultivated, and their granaries very empty. They shall wear elegant and ornamented robes, carry a sharp sword at their girdle, pamper themselves in eating and drinking and have a superabundance of property and wealth — such (princes)

may be called robbers and boasters. This is contrary to the Tao surely."

Ch. 57.　1. "A state may be ruled by (measures of) correction; weapons of war may be used with crafty dexterity; (but) the kingdom is made one's own (only) by freedom from action and purpose."

2. "How do I know that it is so? By these facts: in the kingdom the multiplication of prohibitive enactment increases the poverty of the people; the more implements to add to their profit that the people have, the greater disorder is there in the state and clan; the more acts of crafty dexterity that men possess, the more do strange contrivances appear, the more display there is of legislation the more thieves and robbers there are."

Ch. 58.　1. "The government that seems the most unwise,
Oft goodness to the people best supplies;
That which is meddling, touching everything,
Will work but ill, and disappointment bring."

Ch. 61.　1. "What makes a great state is its being (like) a low-lying, down-flowing (stream); it becomes the center to which tend (all the small states) under heaven."

2. "(To illustrate from) the ease of all females: the female always overcomes the male by her stillness. Stillness may be considered (a sort of) abasement."

3. "Thus it is that a great state, by condescending to small states, gains them for itself; and that small states, by abasing themselves to a great state, win it over to

47

them. In the one case the abasement leads to gaining adherents, in the other case to procuring favor."

4. "The great state only wishes to unite men together and nourish them; a small state only wishes to be received by, and to serve, the other. Each gets what it desires, but the great state must learn to abase itself."

Experience has borne out this statement. Harsh legislation including imprisonment has not solved crime. Education in a broad sense, at an international level, recognizing that man has free will, inculcating principles of human love of neighbor, tolerance and understanding should form the aim of society. Politics does not seem to have solved human problems. On the contrary it has caused wars and has made the poor poorer.

Only the ideal of perfection, in spirituality and in Taoist (and Christian) principles, can lead to perfect harmony. The only perfect ideal is the spiritual one.

Ch. 59.   1. "For regulating the human (in our constitution) and rendering the (proper) service to the heavenly, there is nothing like moderation."

The practice of moderation is advocated particularly in Buddhism and Taoism. This is compatible with modern findings in life science. Inactivity leads to decrease in motivation and degenerative body changes: excess activity leads to stress and psychosomatic disorders.

Ch. 65.   1. "The ancients who showed their skill in practicing the Tao did so, not to enlighten the people, but rather to make them simple and ignorant."

2. "The difficulty in governing the people arises from their having much knowledge. He who (tries to) govern a state by his wisdom is a scourge to it, while he who does not (try to) do so is a blessing."

Ch. 71.   1. "To know and yet (think) we do not know is the highest (attainment); not to know (and yet think) we do know is a disease."

A little knowledge implies much ignorance. Knowledge leads to good and bad use of people and materials. Considerable knowledge leads to understanding particularly when it includes different cultures and transcends cultural and religious barriers.

The principle of keeping the people ignorant is gradually losing ground, but unfortunately the quality of education is generally narrow, rational and confined to one culture and religion.

Ch. 76.   1. "Man at his birth is supple and weak, at his death, firm and strong. (So it is with) all things. Trees and plants, in their early growth, are soft and brittle; at their death, dry and withered."
               2. "Thus it is that firmness and strength are the concomitants of death; softness and weakness, the concomitants of life."

Biological principles require flexibility and adaptation. All branches of life science include these principles; particularly the human nervous system and psychological patterns and responses.

Adaptation of cultures is necessary in changing conditions, for survival. This means the need to change with reasonable limits. Excessive change, however, means death of a culture as well as of a biological system.

Ch. 8.   2. "The sage does not accumulate (for himself). The more that he expends for others, the more does he possess of his own; the more that he gives to others, the more does he have himself."

The principle that what one gives away (materially) one keeps (spiritually) is well known one in Christianity. Material things are owned temporarily, spiritual "riches" and values eternal.

Confucianism and Taoism contain in their philosophy, much that is found in Western society, in Christianity.

CHAPTER 4

HINDUISM AND CREATIVE EVOLUTION

Hinduism is both a religion and a way of life. Its scriptures are the Vedas (Veda means Knowledge) the Upanishads, the Puranas, the Bhagavadgita and others. The Bhagavadgita contains the essentials of Hindu faith. Early Hindu concepts of God involved creation, the sun, thunder, the wind, agriculture, sacrifice and medicine. There appears to have been belief, initially, in a number of Gods. The most important ones were Vishnu or the sun, Indra or God of storm and thunder, Rudra or cloud, Varuna or wind, Agni, which is fire or light, and Krishna, God Incarnate in man. The Vedas were hymns that were composed by many seers, in Sanskrit. Many of the earliest poems were concerned with sacrifice and this involved offerings of soma or wine. The Upanishads were simple stories with a moral.

Offerings of food were given to God, in return for vegetables and fruits, kindly provided through weather, agriculture and vegetation. Just as gods were considered to provide for man, including food and water, so also man was advised in the early

51

Vedas to return gifts to God, in gratitude for what he received. The earliest concept of god related to man's immediate requirements and thus the sun and elements, water, food and wood (for sacrifice) attained supernatural importance. Some early hymns imply the presence of god in the sun, thunder, wind, trees, and in animals; manifestations of creative evolution. Only gradually did there develop a concept of universal god, Vishnu who was later named Krishna. "He" became the most important God and others were considered to be of his substance or essence. The idea of "one numerical god" does not seem to have developed. However, the infinity of god was realized and the various earthly materials were considered creations of the universal, infinite god. The concept of infinity (god being everywhere) led to the understanding that god, unlike man, was not limited in his power or perfect qualities. Many hymns relate to the presence of god in food, drink or animals. God was considered present in material as well as spiritual things. God was primarily the spiritual creator of all things, material and biological. However, he was considered to intervene at special phases in the creative evolutionary process and his intervention was given the name of Avatar or descent.

The ten chief Avatars of Vishnu were as follows:

1. The fish: Matsya. The spirit of God, Vishnu, became a fish, so that he could assist man to be saved from the flood, and carry on Vedic knowledge to the next age. The fish was considered to be the ancestor of man.

2. The Tortoise: Kurma. Vishnu appeared as a tortoise and saved the nectar of immortality. The tortoise was believed to represent a phase in development of animal life. All creatures are descendents of the tortoise, according to tradition.

3. The Boar: Varaha. The earth was covered by the sea and the avatar Varaha brought it to the surface, as "dry land."

4. Man-lion: Narahasinha. The form of a man-lion was assumed by Vishnu, who saved man from an "evil-one."

The appearance of these four avatars was in the first, the "golden age" or satya-yuga, the age of truth.

5. The Dwarf: Vamana. This avatar saved man from the evil demon, Bali who ruled heaven, earth and sky. Vishnu, in the guise of a dwarf, obtained a promise from Bali of all he could cover in three strides. The dwarf became a giant and crossed the earth and sky in three steps.
6. Rama with the Axe: Parashurama. This avatar saved the priestly caste from being overthrown by the warrior caste.
7. The Mild One: Rama. The demon Ravana is defeated by the hero of the Ramayana epic.

These three Avatars occurred in the second or silver age.

8. The Dark God: Krishna. The first avatar of the third or copper age was considered the human incarnation of God.
9. The Teacher: Buddha. The originator of Buddhism and chief founder of meditation. The first avatar in Kali, the iron age.
10. Truth: Kalki. The rebirth of the spirit of truth (satya) shall be followed by its spread throughout the world. All Knowledge converges in this culmination, the "end of days" which is also a new beginning.

Thus there were manifestations of god involving his descent, including a fish, tortoise, a boar, the dwarf, and finally man. These different species represent the main phases of creative evolution.

The eighth incarnation of the series was Krishna, a human avatar. Krishna, however, had human parents and his divine inspiration seems to have been based on his learning. His pronouncements were put together between 500 and 200 A.D. in the Bhagavadgita. It is probable that the contents of the Gita are from various sources and were put together in sequence about this time. The Gita is represented as a story of the battle "mahabharat" and it incorporates a dialoque between Arjuna and Krishna concerning philosophy of living and spirituality.

The concept of god and of divinity in Hinduism implies that god is particularly manifest in his animal and plant creation as a spirit. In earlier writing it appears that the different manifestations were represented as different gods. Development of human understanding of god led to the concept of god as absolute or infinite. This means a unity of god in all his aspects of creation as well as his spiritual essence. Also, he is represented as Brahma, the creator, Vishnu, the preserver of life and the universe, and Siva, destroyer (The Hindu Trinity). There are some who consider that Hinduism involves many single gods: to some extent this may be true among some villagers and uneducated persons. Fundamentally there developed in Hinduism a belief in unity of god. It should not be considered that Hinduism involves worship of animals or plants as such, or as god. God is worshipped through these, indirectly. Similarly, in many religions, representations or images are used to help people meditate on god and these symbols are not worshipped on their own account.

It is proposed in the present summary to deal with the Bhagavadgita and particularly with the sayings of Krishna to Arjuna. Krishna gives advice concerning goodness, honesty, charity, justice, courage, decisiveness and, above all spirituality. The main message in the Gita is that man should become spiritual rather than attached to material things. He should separate himself from the desires and materials of this world and unite with god, who is represented here by Krishna. The context of the story is against the background of an impending battle. This represents the battle of good against evil. The general philosophy of living is described in so far as it affects relations between man and other people; it is stated that man should aim at spirituality and perfection.

It is implied that man is attached to desire and materialism on earth and that this attachment causes man to be imperfect. Perfection is indicated as a quality of spirituality and man is advised to choose the right path, or way. The aim of the individual is to become "one with the Absolute" which is "united with god." This corresponds to the mystic ideal of meditators of other religions. Meditation seems to have been practiced more in Hinduism and in Buddhism than in Western religions. Meditation is encouraged in the Gita and contemplation is urged, on the words and teaching of Krishna. The fundamental ideas of Christianity and Hindu teaching are similar. We should strive to reach the kingdom of heaven, which is spiritual perfection.

Hinduism teaches predestination, but leaves open a possibility of some freedom of human decision. The emphasis on predestination, as in Islam, contrasts with free will, which is the basis of Christianity. Man is considered, however, to have the ability to choose between good and evil and his choice determines his future life. If he is perfect he will become one with the absolute after death, like a drop of water becomes part of the ocean, losing, however, his individuality. If man has not become perfect he is believed to assume a new life in an animal or person depending on how he lives (transmigration of souls). A series of reincarnations may follow a death, each one being determined by previous lives and especially by human behavior. The final life is that of a perfect person, who achieves nirvana after death. This nirvana is a state of bliss and detachment and of not desiring anything of this life. In Hinduism, in the afterlife one becomes part of collective cosmic consciousness, rather than continuing to exist, as an individual personality. The basic principle that determines reincarnation is the law of Karma. This means that good action is rewarded by good and evil action by evil; man has a duty to be good and to fulfill a particular role to play in this life.

Meditation is given prominence in Hinduism and the object is to become one with the Absolute or Brahman (God). During meditation some claim they have reached this state and say "I am Brahman." The question arises whether someone who says "I am Brahman" is setting himself up as a god, independent of the Absolute. If independent being is claimed, that is becoming a god, then the situation is similar to christian "original sin." This Christian concept implies the development of (human) independence of God, in free will. Free will implies that man, unlike animals, is not controlled by instinct, or predestined in his behavior, but is free to make his own decisions.

In life science it is accepted that man can make a decision of his own, that he has free will. It is also realized that there are many genetic and environmental factors which predispose towards human individual patterns of behavior. It is impossible to evaluate the relative importance of these influences and they vary in different persons. From the biological viewpoint, movements of voluntary type can be brought about by stimulating brain cells that form the motor or controlling section of the brain. Evidence shows that decision involves the higher part of the brain, the cerebral cortex. Taking all things into account and considering movement as the main human action, it is probable that less than 4% of all movements involve free will. Even then genetic and environmental influences play a part, and the existence of these, as well as predictability in astrology, may be considered the basis for belief in predestination.

In meditation one aims at losing self-consciousness, sensations, thoughts, memories, desires, etc. and attaining union or oneness with God (the Absolute). A state of consciousness may be reached in which the feeling is one of "nirvana," i.e. detachment, with a sense of being united with the universe and universal thought, while maintaining a minimal degree of "knowing." Complete union with God implies attainment of a state of perfection and is the main objective of Hindus who practice meditation. If the claim "I am Brahman" does not mean literally "I am god" or "I am personal, separate God," then it presumably implies a claim of unity with god, the absolute and infinite. If so, it corresponds to the mystical meditative state reached by some Christians and others. Alternatively it is similar to the claims of Christ to be "one with the father." If the meaning is only "united" then it is implied that there is separateness of some kind but a bond effecting the union. If there is complete union, like a drop of water in the ocean, then there is loss of individuality, and of personal experience. In the case of mystic states and claims such as "I am Brahman" it seems that there is preservation of separate identity and experience. Thus the claim, involving separateness, seems to imply being god and being separate.

The main themes of Hinduism are dealt with in the Bhagavadgita and it is considered, for the purpose of the present investigation, that the Gita is a culmination of the writings forming the Vedas and the Upanishads. It also represents the final step in evolutionary creation, as the Hindu concept of avatar or incarnation of "god in man." It should be understood that physically this is different from the Christian concept since Krishna had a father and mother who were human, whereas Christianity claims that Christ had no human father. The Bhagavadgita describes a discourse between Krishna, who represents god, and Arjuna, general of an army, prepared for battle. Arjuna is undecided whether he should fight and Krishna discusses his duty, philosophy of life, devotion, motivation and the relation between this life and eternity. This forms a background against which Arjuna has to decide his role and duty as a soldier.

The Gita is formed of eighteen chapters and has three main divisions. These are concerned with action without desire, devotion and conscience, and the soul and eternity (Thou and That). Krishna is described as the son of Vasudeva (father) and Devaki (mother) and is said to be the guru of the universe, and god. The series of avatars described in Hinduism culminates in this descent of god to man. From a scientific viewpoint, previous avatars represent stages in creative evolution. Krishna is the final creation and the implication that he is god as well as man is against the background of Hindu thought that god is the maker and the becomer, in all things including man. However it becomes clear as the Gita discourse unfolds that god is present in man (represented by Krishna) but that man is also distinct from god.

The first chapter of the Gita is introductory and deals with preparation for the battle "mahabharat." The second chapter is formed mainly of Krishna's advice to Arjuna. Arjuna has asked Krishna whether he (Arjuna) should fight and Krishna is explaining to him a philosophy of life and of duty in relation to the spiritual background from which man emerged as a created being, material as well as spiritual. Knowledge and understanding form the basis for the initial discussion. In the present examination of the Gita it is probably best to indicate the subjects and to quote extracts.

"With my nature overpowered by thee. Say decidedly what is good for me. I am Thy disciple. Instruct me who have taken refuge in Thee" (2:7).

Arjuna is a Kshatrya, that is, he belongs to the second caste and is a soldier. His indecision is to be considered against a background of his duty, and killing in war is contrary to the purpose of the Brahman or upper class and is considered sinful for them.

"Notions of heat, and cold, of pain and pleasure, are born, O son of Kunti, only of the contact of the senses with their objects. They have a beginning and an end. They are impermanent in their nature. Bear them patiently, O descendent of Bharata" (2:14).

"That calm man who is the same in pain and pleasure, whom these cannot disturb, alone is able, O great amongst men, to attain to immortality" (2:15).

Krishna implies here that material life is finite and little in importance compared to eternity. In human development man's state of self-consciousness became imperfect because of the senses and involvement with material things. Therefore Krishna is indicating that these are not so important as the "real," the unchangable, eternal being.

"That by which all this is pervaded — that know for certain to be indestructible. None has the power to destroy this Immutable" (2:17).

"He who takes the self to be the slayer, and he who takes it to be the slain, neither of these knows. It does not slay, nor is it slain" (2:19).

Eternal Life — being or consciousness — is everywhere, is unchanging and cannot be destroyed. This is the real and important aspect of the universe and one should not speak of spirit being killed. This is because the reality of eternity is much more important than the unreality, mutability and impermanence of life on earth. Furthermore, events are predestined, and not just as we choose to arrange them. So when we speak in real terms we discount human life and death as being of little importance compared to etenal life which cannot be slain. The background of the following verse is similar.

"This is never born, nor does it die. It is not that, not having been, it again comes into being. (Or according to another view: It is not that having been, it again ceases to be.) This is unborn, eternal, changeless, ever-itself. It is not killed when the body is killed" (2:20).

Similarly in the following:

"This Self cannot be cut, not burnt, nor wetted, nor dried.

Changeless, all-prevading, unmoving, immovable, the Self is eternal" (2:24).

One's duty in this life is according to caste and related to background and heredity. In the case of Arjuna it is to fight as a soldier. Each person has a talent to develop and action to carry out in relation to his particular capability. For Arjuna, Krishna advises as follows:

"But if thou refusest to engage in this righteous warfare, then forfeiting thine own Dharma and honor, thou shalt incur sin" (2:23).

"The world also will ever hold thee in reprobation. To the honored, disrepute is surely worse than death" (2:34).

In the verses quoted emphasis is laid both on material and spiritual facets.

"In this, O scion of Kuru, there is but a single one-pointed determination. The purpose of the undecided are innumerable and many-branching" (2:41).

Indecision is an enemy of man whereas will-power and knowledge lead to the "straight path" of action. The purpose of man's activity is here underlined. It is implied that decision is a human function and that man has free-will.

"Thy right is to work only; but never to the fruits thereof.

Be thou not the producer of the fruits of (thy) actions;

neither let thy attachment be towards inaction" (2:47).

Reward and punishment should not be the main reasons for man's behavior. These are represented in animal brains as well as in the human, and animals can be taught to press levers and to learn, etc. for the reward of food or to avoid painful stimuli. A man's understanding of life and its purpose should be beyond this and his motivation should be guided by higher principles, above those in animals. Thus a man should not look for reward nor determine his action and behavior so as to avoid punishment. He should carry out his duties and use his talents to obey the will of God and for the sake of humanity, without expecting a reward. Motivation, depending on reward and punishment only, is primitive.

Arjuna is advised against inaction.

"Being steadfast in Yoga, O Dhananjaya, perform actions, abandoning attachments, remaining unconcerned as regards success and failure. This evenness of mind (in regard to success and failure) is known as control" (2:48).

Tranquillity or evenness of mind facilitates concentration and thus proper mental and physical activity. Concentration and coordination are closely related. Attention is best performed against a background of quiet, and distraction causes inefficiency. Experiments on meditation indicate greater efficiency in physiological functions, especially mental ability, in those who practice regularly. Similarly, favorable results show that yoga (involving controlled muscular posture and exercises) has a beneficial effect on body functions. The achievement of mental tranquillity is to be desired, not only for physiological reasons, but also psychological and psychiatric. Control of sensitivity and mentality as well as reactivity forms the basis for proper adjustments to changes in personal environment.

"When thy intellect, tossed about by the conflict of opinions, has become immovable and firmly established in the self, then thou shalt attain self-realization" (2:53).

A feature of the human mind involving learning, experiences, memory and association, and particularly the subcortical center known as the reticular activating system (RAS), is the possibility of various actions or patterns of behavior from which one may be chosen. The resulting confusion due to indecisiveness has led to stress in man, and this is worsened by the human character of independence of thought and decision. Free will implies that we are capable of choosing a subject or object on which we may think or concentrate. It is not confined to decisions on behavior. This whole field is the same as "original sin" of Christianity. The mentality of attachment to materialism referred to in the Gita, corresponds to Genesis, intelligence leading to knowledge and freedom of choice. The condition of mental tranquillity is the "Kingdom of Heaven" of Christianity.

"The turbulent senses, O son of Kunti, do violently snatch away the mind of even a wise man, striving after perfection."

"The steadfast, having controlled them all, sits focused on Me as the Supreme. His wisdom is steady, whose senses are under control."

"Thinking of objects, attachment to them is formed in a man. From attachment longing, and from longing anger grows" (2:60).

Man, being intelligent, has sometimes pursued pleasure for its own sake and this attachment to pleasure is associated with personal selfishness and dissociation from the interest of the community. It is only by control of human desires and impulses that people's roles in society can be properly achieved. Man's intelligence and emotions have led him to consider "the real" or unchanging, the eternal being who is god, whose principles are unvarying and who is not attached to the changes involved in material things, in time and space. Only in man can pleasure be consciously dissociated from biological purpose. It is only men, among various species, who can knowingly thwart god's will. It is the self-consciousness and natural inclination to earthly, materialist things which comprise the finiteness in nature, the "fall" of man which is the original sin of Christianity.

"But the self-controlled man, moving among objects with senses under restraint, and free from attraction and aversion, attains to tranquillity" (2:64).

"In tranquillity, all sorrow is destroyed, or the intellect of him who is tranquil-minded, is soon established in firmness" (2:65).

"No knowledge (of the Self) has the unsteady. Nor has he meditation. To the unmeditative there is no peace. And how can one, without peace, have happiness" (2:66).

"For the mind which follows in the wake of the wandering

senses carries away his discrimination, as a wind (carries) a boat on the waters" (2:67).

Suffering according to Buddha, is a facet of human desire and activity. The similarity to Buddhism is clear here in tranquillity of mind and freedom from earthly distractions. However, looking at Hinduism as a whole, and particularly the Gita, there is a positive approach rather than a negative one. There is an explanation of the relation between human life and its purpose on the one hand, and eternity on the other. There is a positive theism in contrast with the philosophy of Buddhism. There is emphasis on spirituality, contemplation rather than a state of nirvana, which may be predominantly emotional and self-annihilating.

For man there is a choice between wandering, uncontrolled thought, associated with the pursuit of earthly happiness or the pursuit of the welfare of man, in conjunction with the achievement of the will of the creator, or avoidance of constructive activity through meditation carried to the not- conscious stage.

"That man who lives devoid of longing, abandoning all desires, without the sense of 'I' and 'mine,' he attains to peace" (2:71).

"This is to have one's being in Brahman, O son of Partha. None, attaining to this, becomes deluded. Being established therein, even at the end of life, a man attains to oneness with Brahman" (2:72).

Way of Action

"In the beginning (of creation), O sinless one, the twofold path of devotion was given by Me to this world: the path of knowledge for the meditative, the path of work for the active" (3:3).

The main activities of man can be said to be either physical or mental and the latter are rational or emotional. Action is described in the Vedas as being related to one or other of these. Thus some people are occupied mainly in physical activity, for example in agriculture or industry, whereas others are involved in mental processes of learning and teaching. Also, in relation to mental development there are those who serve by their love for mankind and their services to the community, involving physical and mental care. Human development characteristically exhibits variety in mental ability and interests (as well as in physical appearances) and total human mental progress is dependent on individual contribution. A particular talent for learning, research, or inspiration may be unique, and lack of its use may delay progress in a particular field.

"The Devas (good), cherished by Yajna (good works), will give you desired for objects.

"So he who enjoys objects given by the Devas without offering (in return) to them is verily a thief" (3:12).

The whole question of sacrifice goes back to the beginning of human knowledge of god, as indicated in the vedas. Some early hymns prescribe methods for sacrifice, the use of some wine and the offering of food and of animals. Fires were used to make burnt offerings to god and one of the first names of god was Agni (light or fire).

"Verily by action alone, Janaka and others attained perfection; also, with the view for the guidance of men, thou shouldst perform action" (3:20).

"Whatsoever the superior person does, that is followed by others. What he demonstrates by action, that people follow" (3:21).

"As do the unwise, attached to work, act, so should the wise act, O descendant of Bharata, (but) without attachment, desirous of the guidance of the world" (3:25).

Improvement in agriculture, medicine and education, has involved considerable endeavor. Whereas in some cases advances have led to both good and evil consequences, the general trend in medical areas is towards improvement. There is a close interrelation now evident between principles of medicine, sociology, education and economics and world religion. Only in practice does self-centered interest persist. The objectives of religion, of science and of development of human talents are now understood to be unified and oriented towards a better future for man.

Two main brain mechanisms determine human improvement. One is motivation of man for good, including the good of others. The second is punitive. This is the main feature of primitive religions and legal systems. The degree to which there is a changeover from the latter to the former, that is from punishment to reward, is closely related to the amount of education. Knowledge sets man free, insofar as he acquires rights and comes to know, appreciate and use his talents according to good reason and emotions.

"Better is one's own Dharma (though) imperfect, than the Dharma of another well performed. Better is death in one's own Dharma: the Dharma of another is fraught with fear" (3:35).

The need is emphasized to recognize one's personal role and to seek it with single mindedness. Attachment to thoughts, to personal individual feelings and to desires is distracting and tends to draw attention away from the main purpose of Dharma of one's existence.

"It is desire — it is anger, born of the Rajo-guna; of great craving, and of great sin; know this as the foe here (in this world)" (3:37).

Selfishness, caused by attachment, is a primitive material phase in the development of human mentality and shall hopefully be replaced by community interest, social consciousness or "love of neighbor." There is emphasis both in religions and politics on the relation between the individual and society. Unity of objective can only be achieved in spiritual outlook since materialism results from selfishness, and leads to human divisions and disagreements. Thus the basic purpose of political socialism cannot be achieved, because it has purely material humanitarian grounds. Evidence of the futility of politics as a unifying force is universally available.

Life science and religion are based on the same principles, including maintenance of human life and freedom. Communication and education can be expected to lead to unity in un-

64

derstanding and objectives. To say that ultimate unity shall be based on peace, love, understanding and unselfishness is to echo the principles of Christianity and Hinduism. This is in contrast with Islam which is materialist as well as religious in nature. Islam includes a political system and deals with this life as well as the next. Islam is both materialist and spiritual. It does not frown on attachment to worldly things, nor does it prescribe detachment. Is Islam, being materialist, and oriented towards worldly things, a manifestation of man's natural desire, to turn from God towards earthly, material things? Is Islam thus an expression of the original sin of Christianity? Hinduism and Christianity agree on the evil influence of materialism, desires and resulting anger.

"The senses are said to be superior (to the body); the mind is superior to the senses; the intellect is superior to the mind; and that which is superior to the intellect is He (the Atman)" (3:42).

"Thus, knowing Him who is superior to the intellect, and restraining the self by the Self, destroy, O mighty armed, that enemy, the unseizable foe, desire" (3:43).

Knowledge

"Many are the births that have been passed by Me and thee, O Arjuna. I know them all, whilst thou knowest not" (4:5).

"Though I am unborn, of changeless nature and Lord of beings, yet subjugating My nature I come into being by my own Maya (energy)" (4:6).

"Whenever, O descendent of Bharata, there is decline of Dharma (good) and rise of Adharma (evil), then I body Myself forth" (4:7).

"For the protection of the good, for the destruction of the wicked, and for the establishment of Dharma, I come into being in every age" (4:8).

"He who thus knows, in true light, My divine birth and action, leaving the body, is not born again; he attains to Me, O Arjuna" (4:9).

"Freed from attachment, fear and anger, absorbed in Me,

taking refuge in Me purified by the fire of knowledge, many have attained My Being" (4:10).

The idea that god constantly guides mankind and sends his holy spirit to man for this purpose is shared by Hinduism and Christianity. Also, there is no set time limit in those religions to intervention in this way. Only in Islam is there a claim that Muhammed is the seal of the prophets and this implies that there is no need for further divine guidance. It is in the nature of material and biological things, especially human life, that change occurs. This can be for good or bad. Because of man's own nature of imperfection, he cannot consistently improve, solely by his own nature. Man has only limited knowledge and it requires greater knowledge to lead him in the right path. Ignorance, a necessary character of the human mind, can lead in the wrong direction. Only experience, learning by mistakes, and divine guidance, can provide a lead as to the proper paths to be followed. There is no reason from life science for concluding that divine guidance is finished, in any form or at any particular time or in relation to any person. Recent examples of need for guidance have been contraception and abortion.

"The fourfold caste was created by Me, by the differentiation of Guna and Karma. Though I am the author thereof, know Me to be the non-doer and changeless" (4:13). The fourfold cast system was composed of the Brahman or priestly classes, the military class (Kshatriyas), agricultural (Vaishya) and lower classes (Shudra). This is probably one of the most difficult areas of Hinduism for non-Hindus. It is hopefully tending to decrease in importance nowadays and probably reflects a former situation when it is was of greater importance. In a free society, such as in the West, a person may change from one level of society to another. The levels depend on effort, politics, economics, education, technology and prosperity. In the West, the tendency is to follow the principles of Christianity, that all men are equal in the sight of God. The caste system is based on environment and heredity. Equality relates to spirituality and we all differ materially, physically and mentally. Insofar as the object of society includes justice, human rights and equal opportunity, then there should not be a system in operation which divides man into classes, such as the four-class system of Hinduism. To consider that some people are untouchable is to imply that they are less than other men, subhuman. The presence of the four-caste system in Hinduism leads one to consider that at least one of its aspects is less than perfect, by spiritual standards.

"Some Yogis perform sacrifices to Devas alone, while others offer the self as sacrifice by the self in the fire of Brahman alone" (4:25).

Whereas some people offer sacrifice to god, sometimes through an aspect or manifestation of god, others dedicate their whole being, sensory and motor, to spiritual work. Thus the dedication of the individual and his spiritual offering of his life is recognized in Hinduism as well as in some other religions. This is particularly so in Christianity. Christ was the ultimate in perfection and offered himself in self-sacrifice. The similarity of Hinduism and Christianity extend throughout most aspects of both. This verse further underlines their common mentality.

"Knowledge-sacrifice, O scorcher of foes, is superior to sacrifice (performed) with (material) objects. All action in its entirety, O Partha, attains its consummation in knowledge" (4:33).

"As blazing fire reduced wood into ashes, so, O Arjuna, does the fire of knowledge reduce all Karma to ashes" (4:37).

"The ignorant, the man without Sraddha, the doubting self, goes to destruction. The doubting self has neither this world, nor the next, nor happiness" (4:40).

Knowledge relates to material things, to science, to oneself, to society, and to spirituality. Limited knowledge means that one knows one's own mind and desires and is self-conscious or selfish. Increased knowledge extends to the consciousness of other individuals and to compassion and love of other people through understanding.

A parallel may be made between individual consciousness and that of mankind in general. The parallel includes neurones acting individually in the brain and also in harmony with other neurones. Similarly, for man, society and universal human consciousness. Universal consciousness is more important than that of the individual. Reason, emotions, environment, heredity and mentality lead to judgement which is oriented in relation to the mind of the observer. Personal bias should not apply to evaluation of the standard of achievement or behavior of other individuals. Knowledge between nations and followers of different religions has similar application and the same principle applies as the individual in relation to others.

Renunciation

"Shutting out external objects: steadying the eyes between the eyebrows; restricting the even currents of Prana (breathing out) and Apana (inspiring) inside the nostrils; the senses, mind and intellect controlled; with Moksa (liberation) as the supreme goal; freed from desire, fear and anger, such a man of meditation is verily free forever" (5: 27-8).

The steady state of tranquillity of mind reached by meditation is now known to be desirable for physiological, psychological, psychiatric and spiritual reasons. There is a sub-cortical brain center, the reticular formation, which acts like a thermostat and regulates the activity of the brain. It also serves to focus attention and determines the degree of alertness as well as (one pointed) concentration. Also, it helps in governing excitability of the emotional system (e.g. the limbic system) of the brain and the hypothalamus. The interrelation between meditation and the various bodily systems is now well understood and it is clear that there are psychosomatic interactions between higher rational and emotional levels of the brain and circulation, as well as other bodily systems. The control systems for different physiological functions are integrated and controlled selectively by the reticular formation in conjunction with the cerebral cortex, which contains rational and emotional centers.

The changes from alertness through wakefulness, drowsiness, closed eyes, sleep, etc. are well reflected in the brain waves of the human electroencephalogram (EEG). Comparisons have been made between the EEG in meditation and sleep, coma, anaesthesia, tranquillity induced by drugs, self-hypnosis and other states of the nervous system. Furthermore, a variety of physiological parameters are used simultaneously to identify the relation between meditation and other functional states of the brain. It is well known that concentration or thought or mental tranquillity is affected by sensory input including noise, light, pressure, pain, position, temperature, etc., and it has been shown that minimal input should be attained, so as to record basal cerebral activity or changes resulting from meditation. This is confirmed by electrical recording from the brain, using the EEG. There is a controlling system involving the whole sensory input from the level of the higher centers down to the peripheral receptors such as the eye, ear, or skin and this controlling system involves the reticular formation, sympathetic system, the hypothalamus and the thalamus. This new advance in physiology helps us to understand how meditation effects a lowering of sensitivity and excitability. Furthermore chemical substances, including polypeptides, are released in relation to mental states, emotion and meditation, which further regulate sensitivity. Some of these are encephalins whose main action is to diminish or abolish the sense of pain. Release of these substances in sufficient amount during meditation could serve to explain the anaesthesia often attained by practiced meditators.

Meditation

"For the man of meditation wishing to attain purification of heart leading to concentration, work is said to be the way; for him, when he has attained such (concentration) inaction is said to be the way" (6:3).

"Verily, when there is no attachment, either to sense objects, or to actions, having renounced all purposes, then is one said to have attained concentration" (6:4).

A life science or Western view of concentration contrasts with this. Concentration appears to be determined by the reticular formation (RF) in selecting a subject from store in the cerebral cortex and the degree of concentration is determined by

69

the RF. This center regulates the basal activity of the brain as well as the specific areas for attention to external objects.

"The Yogi should constantly practice concentration of the heart, retiring into solitude, alone with the mind and body subdued, and free from hope and possession" (6:10).

"Thus always keeping the mind steadfast, the Yogi of subdued mind attains the peace residing in Me — the peace which culminates in Nirvana (Moksa)" (6:15).

"When the completely controlled mind rests serenely in the Self alone, free from longing after all desires, then is one called steadfast (in the Self)" (6:18).

Yoga involves controlled body movements and variation in posture in association with activity of cerebral brain cells. Beginning with respiration, the subject practices co-ordination and control as well as concentration on body movements. This is training for nerve cells rather than muscle. Control of mental processes is achieved particularly by practice, whereas in many individuals such control is absent or poor. The processes involved in mental activity do not necessarily involve correlation with movement and an alternative path to mental tranquillity and satisfactory action is by way of learning and knowledge. Physiologically the sensory system is involved in muscle movement, as well as the motor. Sense of position and of movement is subserved by receptors in the joints, tendons, and muscles and nerve cell; sensitivity and action are improved by habitual use. Further, the cerebral sensory system is associated with both sensory and motor aspects of movement, the main action of the body. Much of body activity is voluntary or involuntary movement, and the nervous system responds to changes or to stimuli only by movement or secretion. For peace and tranquillity in the brain both sensory and motor systems should be under control. The sensory input can be diminished or the sensitivity of the brain decreased, but concentration requires attention and is improved by mental and physical practices.

"When the mind, absolutely restrained by the practice of concentration, attains quietude, and when seeing the Self by the Self, one is satisfied in his own Self; when he feels that infinite bliss which is perceived by the (purified) intellect and which transcends the senses, and established wherein he never departs from his real state; and having obtained which, regards no other acquisition superior to that, and where established, he is not moved even by heavy sorrow; let that be known as the state called by the name of Yoga, a state of severance from the contact of pain. This Yoga should be practiced with perseverance, undisturbed by depression of heart" (6: 20-23).

"Abandoning without reserve all desires born of purpose and completely restraining by the mind alone, the whole group of senses from their objects in all directions" (6:26).

"Verily, the supreme bliss comes to that Yogi of perfectly tranquil mind, with passions quieted, Brahman-become, and freed from taint" (6:27).

The unreal, the temporal, that which passes and is not eternal relates to this world and this life. The real or that which matters is eternal and unchanging and has far more importance. It is in association with the important things and with the aspects of perfection and timelessness that relate to the eternal that man gets away from imperfection and strives towards perfection.

"The Yogi, freed from taint (of good and evil), constantly engaging the mind thus, with ease attains the infinite bliss of contact with Brahman" (6:28).

"He who being established in unity, worships me, who am dwelling in all beings, whatever his mode of life, that Yogi abides in Me" (6:31).

The reference to unity with eternal life implies separation from time and space and contemplation of the facets of perfection.

"Verily, the mind, O Krishna, is restless, turbulent, strong and unyielding; I regard it quite as hard to achieve its control, as that of the wind" (6:34).

"The Yogi, striving assiduously, purified of taint, gradually gaining perfection through many births, then reaches the highest goal" (6:45).

Gaining perfection through many births is interpreted, in life science, as chemical and psychological as well as spiritual in meaning. Evolution of chemistry of the brain and of hormones, etc. has accompanied the change from prehuman to human. Differences in people are associated with variations, also, in body chemistry. There is interaction between personality, behavior and chemical changes, and vice versa. Evolution involves decrease in aggression and the attainment of the "perfect human being." Changes in diminution of aggression include alteration in sex and stress hormones in body fluids and tissues.

Knowledge and Realization

"I am the origin and dissolution of the whole universe" (7:6).

"I am the sweet fragrance in earth, and the brilliance in fire am I; the life of all beings, and the austerity am I in ascetics" (7:9).

"Know me, O son of Partha, as the eternal, a seed of all beings, I am the intellect of the intelligent and the heroism of the heroic" (7:10).

The concept of god in Hinduism is considered by many to be pantheistic, that is, present and forming all things. In fact, the concept among Hindus is that it is manifested or continually in operation by maintaining power, movement and life. It is also understood as being unified and coordinated towards integrated design and action.

"The foolish regard Me, the unmanifested, as come into manifestation, not knowing my supreme state — immutable and transcendental" (7:24).

The ignorant regard the deity as they do an ordinary man, considering that he has become manifest in human form. However, god is not changed into material life and the process involving his relationships to man is that he is eternal spirit, unchanged and perfect in comparison with man's imperfection. This verse should be taken with the concept of Hindu avatars in which god intervenes directly at special points in the creative evolution of man. He does not become converted into living material substance but his spirit (Brahman) designs and directs biological change; this is in contrast with the continuation of life which Vishnu maintains, with survival of man and other species. It is implied that there is a difference between creative evolution and maintenance of life. This is obvious biologically, and in the process of changing forms of species, an extra chromosome or other genetic change took place. The special intervention which is claimed for different avatars in Hinduism involved this type of creative change. There is no implication of a human life form being especially created without a father. This contrasts with the Christian claim whereby Christ was conceived by a virgin through the power of God. Presumably the mediation by God formed a Y chromosome in the incarnation of Christ.

"I know, O Arjuna, the beings of the whole past, and the present, and the future, but Me none knoweth" (7:26).

The omniscience of God is believed in Buddhism, Hinduism, Islam and Christianity to include future events. It is sometimes taken to imply predestination, since, if all things are known beforehand, they will become predestined. From a scientific viewpoint it seems that free will and predestination are incompatible.

The Imperishable Absolute

The Blessed Lord said:
"The Imperishable is the Supreme Brahman. Its dwelling in each individual body is called Adhyatma: the offering in sacrifice which causes the Genesis and support of beings, is called (work) Karma" (8:3).

The imperishable or eternal who is God or Brahman is considered to relate to each individual person. It appears from this that God is considered to dwell within each person. The relation may be described as one in which God directs the human mind, while not having complete control over human decisions, because of man's free will. At the same time it can be expected that God's influence is exerted to a varying degree depending on the conformity of the human will with His. Karma (work) relates to the sacrifice, which is a personal dedication to duty. Sacrifice of a person's life action may be offered to God

73

when it corresponds to His will. The greatest sacrifice is one's own human life. It is considered to have been made when his life was offered by Christ.

"And he who at the time of death, meditating on Me alone, goes forth, leaving the body, attains My Being; there is no doubt about this" (8:5).

"Therefore at all times, constantly remember Me, and fight. With mind and intellect absorbed in Me, thou shalt doubtless come to Me" (8:7).

The "being" of eternal life is detachment from material things, and timelessness, in other words, death of this life. The Hindu belief is that on death one becomes "one with the absolute" as a drop of water in an ocean. This implies loss of individual identity. It contrasts with belief in Christianity and Islam in which eternal life is considered to apply to the individual being. The reminder that Arjuna (or man) should fight means that he should fight to concentrate his being, and his effort, in doing what is best and in becoming perfect. The basic relationship between all religions is that man is imperfect and that he should try to become perfect. Man's qualities are said to be finite, in being formed of materials with resulting finite qualities.

"Reaching the highest perfection and having attained Me, the great souled ones are no more subject to rebirth — which is the home of pain, and ephemeral" (8:15).

The doctrine of rebirth or reincarnation is central in Hindu thought. Many lives may be lived, according to this belief, in various animal or human forms, until perfection is reached. States of imperfection are indicated to involve pain and suffering. This is because of man's human sensibility and attachment to things of this world.

Science of God

"And this world is pervaded by Me in My unmanifested form: all beings exist in Me, but I do not dwell in them" (9:4).

"Nor do beings exist in Me (in reality), behold My Divine Yoga;

Bringing forth and supporting the beings, My Self does not dwell in them" (9:5).

"As the mighty wind, moving always everywhere, rests over in the Akas (cloud), know thou, that even so do all beings rest in Me" (9:6).

Whereas the presence of material or movement can be shown scientifically at all the levels of size or radiation, the supernatural power of God is considered to initiate and maintain material and force in nature. In science, one speaks of various levels of magnification or of radiation. In magnification there are levels of the plants, features of landscape, individuals, organs, tissues, cells and fibers, mitochondria and microsomes, DNA and RNA, amino acids and individual atoms. Also, in radiation there are radio waves, visible waves, x-rays, gamma and ultraviolet rays. This applies even at the minutest level and includes specific molecular development in relation to immunity. The concept of the supernatural that relates to God being the source of power is physical, chemical and biological. From a scientific biological standpoint it is considered that the level of action of God is at that of cells and molecules as well as in the individual, community, and universe. The essence which forms the supernatural may be compared scientifically to light, to radiation, or the source of radiation. Thus, there is a close analogy and relation between science, energy and the supernatural which is the source of energy and scientific phenomenon. For the non-scientist or indeed for anyone, the concept expressed in the verse quoted above ("And this world..."), especially the parallel of the wind and clouds, makes some understanding of the supernatural possible. The absolute is infinite or endless in an infinite number of planes, but not formed of material things. Whereas God is believed to be everywhere, in space, He is not present in evil. Evil may exist in the mind but it is still abstract and is a state rather than a material, an attitude rather than a physiological molecular arrangement. The development of human evil is considered in Christianity to be a direct result of free will and the presence in the human mind of the potential for evil (as well as good).

"Glorifying Me always and striving with firm resolve, bowing down to Me, in devotion, always steadfast, they worship Me" (8:14).

"Others, too, sacrificing by the Yajna of knowledge (i.e. seeing the Self in all), worship Me the All formed as one, as distinct, as manifold" (9:15).

Devotion and glory of God are required, at all times according to the Gita. This corresponds to the Christian advice "you should always pray." The basic idea is that one is devoted in thought, motivation, learning, and physical activity and thus life itself is devotion and prayer. The oneness of God relates to continuity in infinity as well as unity of purpose in design. The manifold aspect relates to variety of manifestation in material things and this corresponds to a variety of patterns of control in relation to differences in life, especially in man. It is particularly evident in biological chemical change.

"Whoever with devotion offers Me a leaf, a flower, a fruit, or water, that I accept, the devout gift of the pure-minded" (9:26).

"Whatever thou doest, whatever thou eatest, whatever thou offerest in sacrifice, whatever thou givest away, whatever austerity thou practicest, O son of Kunti, do that as an offering unto Me" (9:27).

The emphasis here is not on the material content of one sacrifice or its value. It is rather on mentality of the giver or the doer. Attitude of mind is what matters and that all things should be done in honor of the creator who provided them and who was the giver of life. The attitude involved is obviously one of love and caring for God and for one's neighbor, who is everyone. Contrasted with this mentality is the hard-mindedness of materialistic man, no matter what his politics or religion is. Only a system or essence or nature which itself is perfect can lead to man's interest in trying to attain qualities of perfection. The greater knowledge one attains and the less one's ignorance, the greater one's ability to teach the less informed. Similarly we can learn and improve and try to increase our good qualities by aiming at the level of greater knowledge and understanding.

"I am the same to all beings — to Me there is none hateful or dear. But those who worship Me with devotion, are in Me, and I too am in them" (9:29).

"If even a very wicked person worships Me, with devotion to no one else, he should be regarded as good, for he has rightly resolved" (9:30).

The simlarity to Christianity is striking. Christ's love of sinners, his compassion, understanding, and forgiveness exemplified by his promise to the thieves on the cross, "This day thou shalt be with Me in Paradise," seems to echo this verse. The attitude in the Gita and in the Gospel is complementary.

"For, taking refuge in Me, they also, O son of Partha, who might be of inferior birth — women, Vaisyas, as well as Sudras — even they attain to the Supreme Goal" (9:32).

Vaisyas are agricultural laborers and they belong to the third of four castes. They are thus considered inferior to the Brahmins and soldiers (Kshatrya). The position of women was considered inferior too in many primitive societies. This was primarily because of the greater physical strength of men. In modern society strength is not considered as important and much physical work is carried out by equipment. This applies also to fighting in war, where missiles largely replace soldiers. Women in some societies tend to be kept separate; they eat after the men have finished and there are many customs which tend to preserve their less privileged position. Domestic duties have been traditionally carried out by women whereas the men foraged for food and animals, usually practiced fighting, agriculture, hunting and religious ceremonies. The tendency has persisted for men to retain their considered superiority. Politics is probably the outstanding example where the vast majority of politicians are men. The more aggressive nature of men has meant that they have taken on the more demanding roles in society. The qualities which have contributed to wars are mainly male ones. Peaceful changes in society and in international attitudes are more likely to result from greater participation by women in social life, religion, organization and politics.

Pervading Power

"Intellect, knowledge, non-delusion, long-suffering, truth, restraint, the external senses, calmness of soul, happiness, misery (pain), birth, death, fear as well as fearlessness, non-injury, evenness, contentment, austerity, benevolence, good name (as well as) ill-fame (these) different kinds of qualities of beings arise from Me alone" (10: 4-5).

Most of the qualities listed are good in nature but a few, perhaps, require a comment. Two of these are misery (pain or suffering) and ill-fame. Long-suffering apparently means unhappiness and ill-fame a bad name or reputation. The whole problem of unhappiness is bound up with pain and suffering and these are dealt with elsewhere (mainly in connection with Buddhism, Christianity and the chapter entitled Consciousness and Stress). It is now clear that much of human suffering is man-made and the result of self-consciousness and selfishness. At the same time there is some suffering especially in genetic conditions, in diseases which were not caused primarily by man. It is questionable whether they are predestined or inevitable. It is evident that genetic abnormalities tend to be prevented, and there is a stability in chromosomal DNA which promotes normal development in man.

Misery (pain or suffering) can be considered to be a part of the created character of mankind insofar as man is imperfect. He is motivated to become perfect; the role of man is to improve society. The ambition which leads him to action in society is unhappiness because of human suffering, disease and social problems. If man were completely happy then he would find little incentive for his proper role in relation to his neighbor, which is mankind. His discontent is an incentive to become involved in abolishment of human suffering, if he shares the Christian mentality.

"I am the origin of all, from Me everything evolves — thus thinking, the wise worship Me with loving consciousness" (10:8).

"The Eternal, the Self-luminous purusa, the first Deva, Birthless, and All-pervading" (10:13).

78

The self-luminous purusa means self-generating light which represents the appearance of God in perceptible form. Reference to representation of God by light, appearing at a certain time, and the source of energy and all life is common to Hinduism and Christianity. It is implied elsewhere in the Gita and the gospel that only some individuals may perceive this light (by means of supra-sensory perception). In other words, it is not the vision of the viewer but special grace or favor from the supernatural deity which confers on some individuals the ability to perceive that which is invisible to others.

"Of manifestations I am the beginning, the middle and also the end; of all knowledge I am the knowledge of the Self, and discussion of disputants" (10:32).

The Gita indicates that Krishna is represented in all earthly manifestations as well as in the sun, moon and so on. He also represents knowledge and truth (Vada). There is apparent conflict between the concept of deity in different parts of the Gita as well as the Upanishads and the vedas. This may be considered to represent an evolution in the human concept. In early writings a pantheistic tendency is evident and this gradually evolves, through avatars (descents or interventions by God) which represent phases of creative evolution. The final, most important, phase is the development of the mind of man. Concepts of universality and unity relate the consciousness of the individual to that of the cosmos or universe and the Absolute. Knowledge and truth lead to understanding of the role of the individual in the cosmos and in society, and to development of motivation for carrying out this role.

Universal Form

"But thou canst not see Me with these eyes of thine; I give thee supersensuous sight; behold My supreme Yoga power" (11:8).

"I see thee of boundless form on every side with manifold arms, stomachs, mouths, and eyes; neither the end nor the middle, nor also the beginning of Thee do I see, O Lord of the universe, O Universal Form" (11:16).

"I see Thee without beginning, middle, or end, infinite in power, of manifold arms; the sun and the moon Thine eyes, the burning fire Thy mouth; heating the whole universe with Thy radiance" (11:19).

"There in the body of the God of Gods, the son of Pandu then saw the whole universe resting in one, with its manifold divisions."

Chapter 11 of the Gita describes the vision of God seen by Arjuna. This vision represented the many manifestations and aspects of divinity. The many arms, eyes, etc. represent the greatness and infinity of God in comparison with man. It is a form which is easily understood but one does not find the use of number to describe God. For example, it is not said that there is one God; it is only implied that God is one in universal cosmic consciousness, creation and manifestation. The vision described is merely to relate material things to the supernatural. The reputation of Hinduism for having many Gods is undeserved. There are many names for the supernatural, the absolute, the creator in relation to different forms of life which god has evolved. But there is not an artificial division of the absolute. Krishna, formerly Vishnu, incorporates all the deities of other names in Hinduism. God has many names and these refer to his creations and characters. Similarly in Islam there are 99 names for god whereas Islam is a strictly monotheistic religion. It implies that there is one god, that is one in number, and its emphasis on this is unique. In Hinduism it is not claimed that there is one god, only that god is one, which means that there is unity in god and he is infinite and not divided, the word absolute being generally used.

"On seeing Thee touching the sky, shining in many a color, with mouths wide open, with large fiery eyes, I am terrified at heart, and find no courage nor peace, O Vishnu" (11:24).

"Having seen Thy mouths, fearful with tusks, (blazing) like Pralaya fires, I know not the four quarters, nor do I find peace; have mercy, O Lord of the Devas, O Abode of the universe" (11:25).

There is an element of awe and fear in these two verses. This is in contrast to the love of god which is almost universal in Hinduism.

The fear is in relation to the finiteness or limitation and the unimportance of man compared to god as well as the power of god and his control over man and man's fate. There is a correspondence, though a minor one, between this attitude of fear and a similar one in Western religion of punishment including eternal suffering in hell.

"So prostrating my body in adoration, I crave Thy forgiveness, Lord adorable. As a father forgiveth his son, friend a dear friend, a beloved one his love, even so shouldst Thou forgive me, O Deva" (11:44).

The theme of forgiveness of sin is present in Hinduism, Islam and Christianity. There is the common implication that in sinning one has turned away from the path of righteousness.

"He who does work for Me alone and has Me for his goal is devoted to Me, is free from attachment, and bears enmity towards no creature — he entereth into Me, O Pandava" (11:55).

One is reminded of the Christian principle of living and forgiving one's enemies, as preached by Christ. There is a direct contrast with Old Testament and Islamic permission to retaliate and return murder for murder. Hinduism and Christianity deal primarily with god, the absolute, spirituality, love, kindness, forgiveness and perfection. Islam deals with religion, politics, law, economics, and materialism. Imperfection relates to human and material things, and perfection to spirituality. The question for the individual is whether to aim at perfection; unless one aims and strives for perfection, one will obviously not reach it. Concern with material things by man, who is self-conscious and selfish, has led to strife and human suffering and furthers his imperfect, finite state.

Devotion

"But those also, who worship the Imperishable, the Indefinable, the Unmanifested, the Omnipotent, the Unthink-

able, the Unchangeable, the Immovable, the Eternal —
having subdued all the senses, even-minded everywhere,
engaged in the welfare of all beings, verily, they reach only
Myself" (12: 3-4).

"He who hates no creature, and is friendly and compassionate towards all, who is free from the feelings of 'I and mine,'
even-minded in pain and pleasure, forbearing, even content,
steady in meditation, self-controlled and possessed of firm conviction with mind and intellect fixed on me — he who is thus
devoted to Me, is dear to Me" (12: 13;14).

The principles of Hinduism are summarized here. They are
devotion, meditation of god, self-control, faith, love, tranquillity, compassion and self-disinterest. One could transpose
Christian principles with these. The emphasis in Hinduism is
on becoming one with the absolute through meditation and
contemplation. In Christianity the emphasis is one loving one's
neighbor, on prevention of suffering, on healing, on social welfare and on compassion and the message is underlined by the
suffering of Christ and his life sacrifice.

The Mind and Knowledge

"The great Elements, Egoism, Intellect, as also the Unmanifested, the ten senses and the one (mind), and the five objects of the senses, desire, hatred, pleasure, pain, the ag-
gregate, intelligence, fortitude — the body has been briefly
described with its modifications" (13: 5-6).

The whole relationship between a person's mind as a subject
and his body and the environment as objects may be conceived
as two separate parts or a unified whole. The existence and
function of one part depends on the other. Thus the mind cannot develop sensation without a body or an environment. However, the environment exists independently of the mind. In
relation to higher functions of the mind, intelligence, emotions
and reason, experience, perception and a sensory system are
required. The division, however, between subject and object is
partly artificial, whereas they form a continual or unified phy-

siological entity. The question whether the mind of man can exist apart from an intact brain, etc. is a difficult one. There is evidence that the mind, or at least an experiencing being, can exist separately from the body, though connected by a thread, for example in astral projection.

"The renunciation of sense-objects and also absence of egoism: reflecting on the evils of birth, death, old age, sickness and pain" (13:8).

This verse relates to the basics of Buddhism and is reminiscent of the statement by the Buddha that birth, death and sickness, etc. involve suffering and that this can be avoided by withdrawal of the attachment of senses to desires. Buddhist meditation and principles are summarized elsewhere in this book and it will be seen that the basic Buddhist philosophy involves some degree of negativity of mental action, meditation and avoidance of human problems.

"Free from pride and delusion, with the evil of attachment conquered ever dwelling in the self, with desires completely receded, liberated from the pairs of opposites known as pleasure and pain, the undeluded reach that Goal Eternal" (15:5).

This verse summarizes the basis for a spiritual existence, including detachment from materialism, and is similar to meditation in the mysticism of all religions.

Divine and Non-Divine

"Fearlessness, purity of heart, steadfastness in knowledge and Yoga; almsgiving, control of the senses, Yajna, reading of the Sastras, austerity, uprightness" (16:1).

"Non-injury, truth, absence of anger, renunciation, tranquillity, absence of calumny, compassion to beings, uncovetousness, gentleness, modesty, absence of fickleness" (16:2).

"Boldness, forgiveness, fortitude, purity, absence of hatred, absence of pride, these belong to one born for a divine state, O descendent of Bharata" (16:3).

"Ostentation, arrogance, and self-conceit, anger as also harshness and ignorance belong to one who is born, O Partha, for an asurika (evil) state" (16:4).

"(The evil say) This today has been gained by me; this desire I shall obtain; this is mine, and this wealth also shall be mine in future" (16:13).

The whole question of human attachment to material things is an important and basic component of the Gita. It is based on objects, perception and sensation combined with pleasure; evolution of this human attachment depended on man developing a form of self-consciousness whereby he recognized his separateness and independence and could consciously distinguish between pleasure and displeasure. This state of mind or attitude meant that man consciously desires earthly things and also uses his free will for decision making. Much of the Gita is therefore virtually the same as the Christian concept of turning away from God to material things and desiring them rather than God. Christians called this (human mentality and) turning away from god, original sin. It depended both on free will and knowledge of good and evil. It meant the presence in man's mind of a potential for evil. The very presence of a potential is evil in itself according to Christianity. In Islam original sin and implied free will and imperfection have not been accepted. The attitude in Islam to materialism is that man is directed to attachment and to lawful and reasonable use of earthly materials and also that he is justified in desires providing they do not lead to law breaking or sin.

"Self-conceited, haughty, filled with the pride and intoxication of wealth, they perform sacrifices in name, out of ostentation, disregarding ordinance" (16:17).

It is implied here that one cannot properly "serve" god and man. One is reminded of the difficulty, in Christ's words, for a rich man to get to heaven; in other words there is no choice between materialism and God.

"Triple is this gate of hell, destructive of the self; lust, anger and greed; therefore one should forsake these three" (16:21).

"He who setting aside the ordinance of the scripture acts

84

under the impulse of desire, attains not to perfection, nor happiness, nor the Goal Supreme" (16:23).

Control of human desires relating to material things forms important aspects of Hinduism and Christianity. Control of human appetites is encouraged by spirituality whereas attachment to material and earthly desires leads to habituation.

"Serenity of mind, kindliness, silence, self-control, honesty of motive — this is called the mental austerity" (17:16).

The emphasis is on mental attitudes: not on deeds or on material things, nor does it relate to precise laws, behavior or economics. The ideal mentality is close to spirituality but relatively unrelated to materialism or capitalism.

Renunciation

"Of Brahmanas and Kshatryas and Vaisyas, as also of Sudras, O scorcher of foes, the duties are distributed according to the Gunas, born of their own nature" (18:41).

"Prowess, boldness, fortitude, dexterity and also not flying from battle, generosity and sovereignity are the duties of the Ksatriyas, born of (their own) nature" (18:43).

"Agriculture, cattle-rearing, and trade are the duties of the Vaisyas, born of (their own) nature, and action consisting of service is the duty of the Sudras, born of (their own) nature" (18:44).

"Devoted each to his own duty, man attains the highest perfection" (18:45).

"The Lord, O Arjuna, dwells in the hearts of all beings, causing all beings, by His Maya, to revolve, (as if) mounted on a machine" (18:61).

Predestination seems to be implied in this verse. The general attitude is that man is bound by his nature, his cast, his upbringing, heredity and environment. There is considerable emphasis on predestination in both Hinduism and Islam. This is probably explained by the recognition by primitive man of repetitive patterns including daily, monthly and annual cycles in the universe and in nature. It can be argued from some passages in Hinduism and Islam that free will exists. For example, Arjuna may be considered free to choose to fight, or not to. However, in this verse it is indicated that his decision is predestined. A similar attitude of belief is apparent in the Koran.

Science accepts free will and does not accept "predestination" except in relation to physical and chemical events. The influence of heredity and environment is accepted by science but the role of man is fundamentally free in thought and action and this freedom is an essential quality of the nature of man. Man as a machine relates to muscles, joints, nerve cells and glands. The human brain has evolved beyond the automatic instinctual behavior of animals. Human consciousness, intelligence, learning, memory and free will are accepted in psychology as important attributes of the human mind. Free will is the main aspect of human intelligence which allows man to use his talents and to choose his vocation for their development. In general predestination is an ancient belief of tribal societies. In these it helps to keep the "masses," especially the lower classes, under control. They are told all things are the will of God, and that they must obey God's will. The prosperous, meantime, exploit the poor, in primitive societies. Free will is accepted and practiced in developed (and Christian) societies. There are degrees of variation in freedom according to politics and in some cases politics and religion operate as one. Where this occurs there is limitation of human freedom. Totalitarian governments so limit human freedom by laws that there is very little (left) for man to decide. It is probably not a coincidence that countries which allow human freedom and civil rights are both Christian and modern. They tend to be prosperous and materialistic because man has used his talents. Totalitarian states inhibit individual freedom and development and the people are usually uneducated, or their education is limited, and local in nature.

CHAPTER 5

BUDDHISM, SUFFERING AND MEDITATION

One thing I teach, said Buddha, "Suffering and the end of suffering; it is just ill and the ceasing of ill that I proclaim." The meditative approach, however, which he adopted at that time (sixth century B.C.) was essentially ineffective in physical healing since disease is generally not psychosomatic. The philosophy of meditation developed by Buddha, and of living and behavior, had many advantages, particularly social and psychological. Physical healing was not feasible then, since life sciences had not developed. Medical mentality was to be based on rationality, research, positivity and principles of Christianity — the formula for progress and Western civilization. Healing was to substitute for meditative withdrawal and love of neighbor and for oriental detachment from earthly desires, people and things.

"Buddha," from the Sanskrit root Budh, meaning to be awake and know, was born in Lumbini, South Nepal (then North India); around 563 B.C. according to Western scholars. Named Siddhartha Gautama, he belonged to the Sakya clan,

TABLE 1

CAUSES OF SUFFERING

Personal	Injury, physical and mental illness; Mood, Anxiety, Sleep, Guilt, Frustration. Property loss or damage. Legal. Employment loss, loss of function, Grief, loss of family, friend etc. Reputation, Accommodation, Education.
Family	Life events similar to personal, Physical or psychological disease, death, status change, divorce, change or deficient housing, disputes, legal problems, property.
Friends and Relations	Loss through Death, Illness, Marriage. Life events. Departure. Disagreements.
Community/ Social	Employment, Social change, Reputation: Defamation, Legal event, Epidemic, Amenities, Health, Education, Transport, Communications, Electricity, Water.
National/	War, Political Upheaval, Economic/Industrial Problems,
Racial/	Strikes, Prejudice, Bigotry.
Religious/	Prosecution, Discrimination, Natural Disaster.
International	Climate, Starvation, Injustice, Repression, Punishment.

Causes of suffering listed on a personal, family, community and national basis. In general they are based on a materialistic attachment of man. The latter is contrary to the principles of spirituality of Hinduism, Buddhism and Christianity.

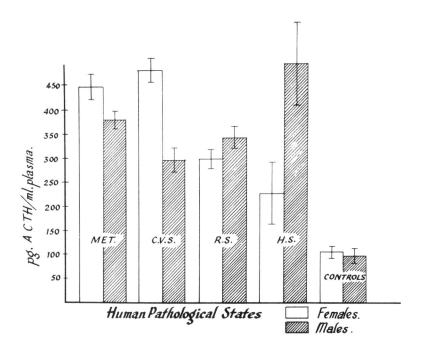

Figure 4

Stress hormone ACTH and diseases. According to the Buddha, being born, being ill, becoming old, and dying all involve suffering. These high blood levels of stress hormone were found in human diseases in our laboratory. They reflect a scientific measure of stress and suffering.

Met., METABOLISM; C.V.S., Cardivascular system; R.S., respiratory system; H.S., hemopoietic system.

89

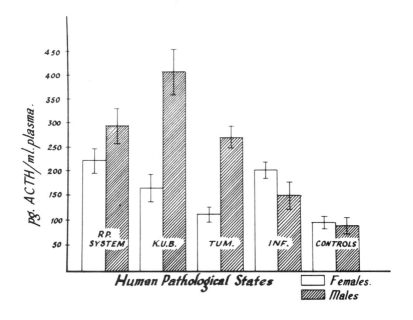

Figure 5

Stress hormone ACTH and diseases. Blood levels of the
stress hormone ACTH in human diseases. These are
elevated in diseases of the various body systems.
R.P., reproductive system; K.U.B., kidney, urinary bladder;
Tum., tumors; inf., infections.

and was a prince or lord. He renounced family wealth and inheritance and became the founder of Buddhism.

Buddhism is described by some as a philosophy and by others as a religion. The prophet of Buddhism, Siddhartha Gautama, developed a technique of meditation which allowed him to reach a state of tranquillity or nirvana. Hinduism was dominated at the time by the Brahmins or priests and the upper class. They believed that their sacrifice controlled the universe, including the gods who were considered responsible for the various happenings on earth and elsewhere. The mode of sacrifice was precisely defined in the Vedas and the Brahmins' superior position in Indian society was due to the power which they claimed to possess and the secrets of ritual sacrifice. Meditation had been carried out before the time of Buddha and there were practices and ceremonies in operation which followed vedic hymnal writings. The development of detailed ceremonies caused a separation between Brahmins and the ordinary people and overemphasis on ritual was beginning to alienate some from Hinduism.

Meditation and principles of morality form the central themes of Buddhism. The meditation was oriented primarily towards mental training, concentration and mind control so that its objectives complemented those of morality which depend primarily on a mental attitude. The primary aim of Buddhism is the development of a mental attitude. In practice only a minority develop sufficient competence in meditation to reach the stage of nirvana. However, the stages of meditation involve a clearing of the mind of earthly thoughts and desires before the stage of nirvana can be attained. The whole process by which the Buddha (teacher) reached the "state of mind" of nirvana involved a progressive process. This involved elimination of thoughts and desires, with eventual attainment of a "not-conscious" state.

The concepts of Buddhism were developed, not alone along several general principles, but also against the specific background of India at the time. Religion had become synonymous with ritual and sacrifice, and it became clear to Buddha that the basic principles of proper living required knowledge, wisdom, speech and action and above all proper attitude. Thinking, reason, emotion, determination, mental concentration and relaxation were all processes that required practice. The theme of Buddhism implied a recognition of early development of man, particularly of human intelligence. It was recognized that man suffers distress in birth, and other aspects of his life. Suffering was basic in determining Buddha's philosophy of life. Distress is similar to a word from Genesis for the condition of man whereby human mental intelligence and sensitivity outstripped that of other species, and man is therefore more subject to stress and strain. The regime recommended in Buddhism involved learning, understanding, knowing, being wise, meditating, behaving, etc., all of which determine human morality and behavior. Originally Buddhism was not a religion. There was no theology or belief in life after death. Gradually there developed changes in belief, akin to those of Hinduism, whereby Buddha became deified through a process of belief that he was an avatar or descent of the holy spirit of god. As time went by more teachers or Buddhas were honored in sainthood (especially in the Hinayana form of Buddhism).

The emphasis in Western thinking on Buddhism is on meditation. The mental exercise known as transcendental meditation is derived from both Hinduism and Buddhism. The process is isolated from the context of philosophy and religion and is used primarily for mental relaxation. In Buddhism meditation is mental training and exercise and the process is one of development of the human mind; it is physiological, psychological and social. It recognizes the basic function of the mind similarly to modern life sciences and it prescribes processes aimed at improving concentration, relaxation, knowledge and memory. It is implied in both Hinduism and Buddhism that distress or suffering result from an attitude of mind which is "attached" to earthly things by desires. The process of detachment is a basic recommendation in these religions, for the attainment of freedom from distress. The general principles of causation of human distress proposed by Buddhism are similar to those described in the Bhagavadgita.

They are also basic tenets of Christianity. Thus these three world religions have this in common, that they associate evil with desires which are not sufficiently controlled and with attachment to material or non-spiritual things. In this way they are based on fundamentals which are the same. Islam, in contrast to the others, includes material attachment, politics, law and economics and is thus a way of life as well as a religion.

Mental training in Buddhism requires that the senses be withdrawn from consideration of objects and desires. For mental tranquillity one requires a quiet atmosphere, so that one is not distracted. Diminished light or even semi-darkness is more conducive to meditation and mental concentration than is bright sunlight. The practice of meditation is usually followed in monasteries or in remote areas or in the quiet corner of a room. The initial objective is to avoid sensory disturbances. Posture is modified and the sitting position is adopted on crossed legs. This diminishes sensory output, including postural impulses. Also, it diminishes the need for muscle tone and the resultant relaxation eases the tension and lessens the sensation in voluntary muscles. Further steps require clearing the mind of all thoughts and memories followed by concentration. Practice is necessary to keep the mind free of distractions. To facilitate the getting rid of multiple thoughts or the "flight of ideas" (which is the common attribute of the human mind, in its poorly controlled state), a process of one pointed concentration is practiced. This involves concentration on a mental image; the image may be a circle or any shape or object. Also, concentration is facilitated by a mantra, that is a word repeated regularly. The word most commonly used is "Om," a Hindi word meaning peace; but different words, usually monosyllabic, are used. The basis for their use is the induction of regular rhythm in the speech and auditory centers of the brain, and their association areas. The mantra and visual object are then cleared from the mind, leaving it blank. The subject is conscious of meditating at this stage. Finally, practiced individuals may reach a further phase which is "not-conscious." This phase involves a feeling of detachment from this world and a resulting calm or tranquillity. This is accompanied by an emotional sensation of pleasantness and oneness with the universe or cosmos. There is a difference between Buddhist meditation and Hindu in that Buddhism aims at a stage further. This is the "not-conscious" phase, when the subject may not even feel pain. In Hinduism oneness with the Absolute is the main aim and therefore this is a theistic form of meditation, whereas Buddhism may be atheistic. In practice, however, the two forms overlap and Buddhism may be theistic or even contemplative. Buddhist meditation is usually practiced in monasteries by monks; these are people who visit the monastery for a time, generally in their early adult life, for a few months or longer. Proficiency at mental training and meditation generally takes many years until ability to reach the stage of "not-consciousness" is attained. For the layman a less ambitious program is usually followed, whereby one or two sessions of meditation are practiced each day and these do not usually progress beyond contemplation. Buddhism, unlike Christianity, discourages all attachment including love of people, and thus lacks the basic principle "love thy neighbor" taught by Christ. Love involves suffering since love may involve separation. Suffering may thus be physical or psychological, being due to injury, disease or grief for one absent or departed or remorse, compassion, anxiety or depression. The Western approach to suffering is by life science and rationality rather than an emotional or negative reaction. Suffering may involve normal or abnormal mental responses, imagination, deletion or substitution of ideas.

A Buddhist theory concerning the causes of suffering involved the twelve origins. These included ignorance, mentality of previous existence, self-consciousness, relation of mind to body senses (six, including mind), attachment to this life, feeling or sensation, desire, striving for oneself and existing or being. The two remaining causes of suffering relate to the future life, and are aging and rebirth in another organism. The sequence of causes described involved proposed previous living, the present life and a further life; thus the whole process of suffering is considered as continual. There is emphasis laid on previous and future lives.

TABLE 2

PREVENTION AND TREATMENT OF SUFFERING

Personal	Avoidance of accidents, care, education, legislation, consideration for others, preventive medicine, medicine/surgery, environment, understanding, compassion, insurance, social security, thrift, behaviour, planning, industry, leisure, diet, exercise, religion.
Family *Friends* *Relations*	Similar to personal: Medicine, Economic measures, Legal protection.
Community/ *Social*	Organization, Opportunities, Education & leisure facilities. Mentality & attitude, Social responsibility, Humanity.
National/ *Racial/* *Religious/* *International*	Media & communications, Planning, Politics and administration, Social welfare, Health & educational facilities, Environment & media, Tolerance. Knowledge & understanding, Charity, Culture, Tradition, Attitude, Experience, Progress, Work, Industry, Leisure facilities, Legal system and Government.

Social, religious and medical aspects underline the importance of personal relationships in prevention of suffering. Christianity and Chinese religions place considerable emphasis on these relationships.

95

The processes of learning, memory, self-consciousness, sensation, desire and appetites are understood in modern biology and there is fundamental agreement between the doctrines of Buddhism concerning mental stress and modern neurophysiology and psychology. To imply that human stress depends on the presence of the human senses and intelligence is to reiterate the Buddhist concept that becoming or existing leads to distress. This implies that human life is susceptible to stress, that the human brain is especially sensitive. Meditation, involving detachment, as a method of avoiding the sensation of human suffering, is a protective and negative approach. However, Buddhism has positive facets also, other than meditation. The positive approach involves mental training, wisdom, understanding, and standards for human behavior and morality.

The basic content of Buddhism concerns living and may be termed philosophical rather than religious. A good deal of emphasis is placed on ignorance as a cause of human suffering. Ignorance is lack of knowledge and implies the presence of intelligence and limitation of knowledge and understanding. The meaning of ignorance in Buddhism is that the individual has only some knowledge and that this relates mainly to himself. He knows his own feelings and appetites. He realizes his individuality and has become self-conscious. It is the exaggeration of self-consciousness and the resulting selfishness which lie at the center of Buddhism. In this Buddhism is based on the early development of man, especially of human consciousness, and associated stress. Christianity and Buddhism have this theme in common, that humanity is imperfect and this is due to man reaching a stage of intelligence but also being limited in his knowledge and understanding and therefore compassion and love of neighbor.

The centrality of stress as a concept in Buddhism and Christianity is evident from physical, psychological and scriptural viewpoints. There is a tradition common to Buddhism and Christianity concerning congenital stress. Buddha was believed to have been born from his mother's hip or side. Indian heroes Aurva, Prithu, Mandhatri and Kakshivat were said to be born

TABLE 3

SUFFERING: Further aspects and factors to be considered

Material resources,
Intelligence, learning, knowledge, memory,
Education, social resources, humanity,
Desires, prudence, motivation,
Selfishness, materialism,
Society, understanding of others,
Free will, thinking, foresight, consideration,
Environment, history, aggressiveness,
Experience, religion, mentality, self-control,
Sensitivity, social interaction, emotions,
Maturity, development, initiative,
Ambition, power, ideology,
Empathy, compassion,
Tolerance, patience,
Social work, charity,
Research in medicine, psychology.

These aspects of suffering further underline the social factors and the susceptibility of man to suffering because of his intelligence and free will. 'Man's inhumanity to man' clearly plays a major role. Old testament writings condoned 'an eye for an eye' and thus human suffering. Christianity aims to diminish or abolish physical and mental suffering.

respectively from the thigh, hand, head or armpit miraculously. In Genesis it is indicated that women (represented by Eve) would bring forth children in congenital distress. Research findings in our laboratory support psychosomatic stress or strain as a cause of human congenital stress or difficulty in labor. We have found that there is a direct relation between blood levels of the stress hormones ACTH and cortisol (in late pregnancy) and duration of human labor. Hormone levels were measured before the onset of labor; thus they were not affected by labor itself, but reflected mental stress before it began. Such stress is considered in Christianity to be due to disobedience to God. The meaning of disobedience in Genesis is absence of obedience (contrast with Moslem which means obedient to God). This came about by development of human intelligence, free-will and independence in decision of God's will. Stress of human responsibility (in decision) thus caused in man, was reflected by congenital stress.

The "Way" in Buddhism is that which leads to prevention of suffering (in contrast with meditation, which is less positive). The "Way" involves wisdom and understanding, morality and mental training which are necessary to prevent human suffering. Perfect wisdom is said to be dependent on perfect mentality and intention. These two mental attributes belong to the eight branches of the eightfold path which forms the way of deliverance. Perfection in speech, action, living and effort are said to lead to morality and proper human behavior. The other two branches are attention and meditation and these lead to normal control and concentration. The aspects of the eightfold path are opposites of the causes of human suffering. Thus, wisdom is the opposite of ignorance and concentration the opposite of distraction and uncontrolled thoughts. Also, perfection in human speech and action is contrary to human imperfection. The objective of the eightfold path is the attainment of perfection. The word often used in describing speech, action, etc. is "right"; however, the word 'perfection' is probably closer to the original texts. A perfect viewpoint is the central theme and objective of the eight branches described. This means mentality, outlook, attitude, emotional state, mental approach and sensitivity, excitability and responsiveness. The main functions of the human brain are involved and include learning, intelligence, decision, free will, memory, understanding, correlation, attention, alertness, and mental control. The exercises prescribed in Buddhism for mental training center around man's relation to himself and to his neighbor. This determines his behavioral pattern. The function of the eightfold path is to give man self-control, to help him decide on suitable behavior and to carry out his decision by will power. He is encouraged to have a proper understanding of man in relation to humanity and the universe. He is to consider the unimportance of man, the short duration of his life, his limitation in goodness and his liability to suffering. Buddhist mental training stabilizes man's mind so that he does not become unduly enamored of his neighbor or upset by disturbing events. The order in which some Buddhists consider the eightfold path are: attention, meditation, will, effort, speech, action, living, and mentality. Mentality may be considered the summation and objective of all the others and determines personality.

The central theme in Buddhism is thus perfect mentality. The eightfold path should be considered as commandments. It includes a process of mental exercise and training for the good of the individual and of society. Attention is concentration on the object of consciousness. It is a function of the human mind and determined by alertness. The level of alertness is known to be determined by the subconscious center, the reticular activation system. This regulates the degree of attention, the subject of one pointed concentration as well as restfulness and sleep. Thus, the reticular system is the most important subconscious area involved in mental exercises. In the process of attention one is expected to practice sensation as an exercise in mind development and control. Thus, one feels a sense of position of lying, standing or sitting and one concentrates on the position of an arm or foot. In Buddhism one is encouraged to regard the body as impermanent and unimportant. It is formed of matter; earthly, of little consequence, temporal, and attached to desires. It is recommended that one meditate on death as the natural end of life. One should develop a transcendental and detached viewpoint towards the body; one should control thoughts, associations, distractions and desires. One practice that was recommended, in relation to death, was that of visualizing corpses in various stages of decay, from that of slight decomposition to skeletons with little or no flesh. Such a practice was carried out, at one time in cemeteries, but mental images may be substituted for real bodies.

Buddhism and Christianity have in common the development of new attitudes and improvement of mentality. Communal living, the development of speech, with increase in communication and interdependence, knowledge of death, grief, illness, injury, physical handicap and the sharing of understanding led to human compassion. Suffering and sharing of the human condition led to an appreciation that man is not alone in having problems. These are universal in man and are physical, medical, psychological and psychiatric. The universality of man's unhappiness and imperfection is admitted in Buddhism, Hinduism, and Christianity. In particular the reason for this condition has been ascribed to self-consciousness and complete understanding. These religions have furthered development of human altruism as an attitude. Hindu stories give instances of extreme unselfishness and these were communicated to encourage charity and compassion in the individual. One is reminded of the Good Samaritan and the Christian attitude in the gospels, which became the antithesis of precepts from the Old Testament. The recognition of the need for compassion was highlighted by Christ's alleviation of suffering, by healing the sick and also by his own suffering. Christ's sacrifice in offering his life on behalf of mankind could be accepted in principle in Buddhist philosophy, against the background of unselfishness and self-sacrifice. Above all, personal experience and meditation of suffering increase understanding between the individual and society. The main objective of Buddhism may be said to consider human suffering and to derive a philosophical attitude from it. Christianity extends the principle of loving people beyond the limit set by human selfish thought. In Christianity, mentality relates spiritually to the creator, as well as to mankind. Thus, it can be considered to be primarily a religion, in comparison with Buddhism which, according to many, is primarily a philosophy.

There are ten Buddhist precepts which are prescribed for human moral behavior. Their existence is justified in view of the general inadequacy of the individual to know how precisely one would conform to society. Buddhist precepts are like the Christian commandments; a general guide to what should, and more often what should not, be done. They tend to be taken more literally in Buddhism, and "thou shalt not kill" relates (in Buddhism) to the killing of animals as well as man. This extends to the prohibition of meat on special days. Buddhist precepts are described as ten meritorious actions:

1. To abstain from killing is good,
2. To abstain from theft is good,
3. To abstain from illicit sexual relations is good,
4. To abstain from lying is good,
5. To abstain from intoxicating drugs and liquor is good,
6. To abstain from evil-speaking is good,
7. To abstain from hard and hurtful words is good,
8. To abstain from covetousness is good,
9. To abstain from cruelty is good,
10. To understand correctly is good (Majjhima Nikaya).

Change or impermanence is a central belief in Buddhism. This implies suffering and also precludes belief in an eternal individual soul. To say that change and impermanence characterize the universe and particularly human existence is almost the same, in implication, as saying that movement is a central feature of the universe and of life. From the point of view of eternal life the concept is similar to that relating to the "unreal in Hinduism." The unreal means that which has impermanence. It implies constant movement and chemical interchanges, including physical changes. That which is real by contrast is, in Hinduism, the absolute or universal deity. In Buddhism most writings do not presume the existence of such an everlasting being. Also, the presence of a human eternal soul is not believed, in Buddhist philosophy. It is argued that the composition of the body keeps changing so that there is no permanence in physical or chemical properties. From this it is deduced that no aspect of the body is permanent or potentially eternal. The absence of belief in an individual soul distinguished Buddhism from Christianity, Hinduism, and Islam. In Buddhism there is no expectation of a next life, or heaven, or of hell. In contrast to other religions Buddhism teaches that reward and suffering follow, and result from, behavior in this life. Thus, one who follows the "way," the eightfold path, and attains perfect mentality, behaves and speaks normally and is happy in conforming to his role in this life. Evil is considered to bring suffering, not alone to one's neighbor, but to one's self.

Memory is considered very important in relation to mental ability and self-discipline in Buddhism. Memory practice is carried out and this involves recalling to mind the events of the day, in reverse, or those over a longer period. It includes evaluation of one's behavior and attitude so that one can assess progress or otherwise in mind control and behavior. One examines one's attitudes, likes and dislikes, activities and speech. The process corresponds to the Christian one of examination of conscience.

In Buddhism Karma is the philosophy of causation running through previous and present lives, and determining the soul's transmigration, and the type of animal or person to be occupied by the soul after birth. Buddhism proclaims the existence of individuals in previous lives, and the principle of determination through them of present happiness or unhappiness. Individuals sometimes claim to remember portions of past lives and the evidence appears to support their claims. If they were good in past lives this is supposed to lead to happiness in the present life. Whereas evil leads to unhappiness. The principle of reward and punishment operates through a sequence of existences. Behavior in the present life determines whether the "consciousness" corresponding to the soul migrates after death into a pleasant or unpleasant species.

The "transmigration" of consciousness is quite different from that in Christiantiy and Islam where an individual soul is believed to be rewarded or punished. No experience of "transmigration" of souls into animals seems to be authenticated. In

102

Buddhism transmigration of consciousness is considered to allow an individual to improve in a series of lives, and eventually to reach perfection in a final human life. Death is then followed by nirvana, which is a state of detachment from material desires and sensations, as well as of tranquillity and happiness. This state corresponds, in general, to the Western idea of life after death. In Christianity, however, there is no doctrine of transmigration of consciousness or reincarnation. The evidence of many individuals who recover from near death appears to support the Western belief of survival of individual consciousness as well as states of pleasure or displeasure.

The following Twelve Principles were drafted By Christmas Humphreys as a summary of Buddhism, for the Buddhist Society: London, in 1945. They were approved by leading Buddhists in Burma, China, Japan, Tibet and Ceylon.

Twelve Principles of Buddhism

1. Self-salvation is for any man the immediate task. If a man lay wounded by a poisoned arrow he would not delay extraction by demanding details of the man who shot it, or the length and make of the arrow. There will be time for ever-increasing understanding of the Teaching during the treading of the Way. Meanwhile, begin now by facing life, as it is, i.e. learning always by direct and personal experience.

2. The first fact of existence is the law of change or impermanence. All that exists, from a mole to a mountain, from a thought to an empire, passes through the same cycle of existence — i.e. birth, growth, decay and death. Life alone is continuous, ever seeking self-expression, in new forms. "Life is a bridge — therefore build no house on it." Life is a process of flow, and he who clings to any form, however splended, will suffer by resisting the flow.

3. The laws of change applies equally to the "soul." There is no principle in an individual which is immortal and unchanging. Only the "Namelessness," the ultimate Reality, is beyond change, and all forms of life, including man, are manifestations of this Reality. No one owns the life which flows in him

103

any more than the electric light bulb owns the current which gives it light.

4. The universe is the expression of law. All effects have a cause and man's soul or character is the sum total of his previous thoughts and acts. Karma, meaning action-reaction, governs all existence, and man is the sole creator of his circumstances and his reaction to them, his future condition and his final destiny. By right thought and action he can gradually purify his inner nature, and so by self-realization attain in time liberation from rebirth. The process covers great periods of time, involving life after life on earth, but ultimately every form of life will reach Enlightenment.

5. Life is one and indivisible, though its ever-changing forms are innumerable and perishable. There is, in truth, no death, though every form must die. From an understanding of life's unity arises compassion, a sense of identity with the life in other forms. Compassion is described as "the law of laws — eternal harmony" and he who breaks this harmony of life will suffer accordingly and delay his own Enlightenment.

6. Life being One, the interests of the part should be those of the whole. In his ignorance man thinks he can successfully strive for his own interests, and this wrongly directed energy of selfishness produces suffering. He learns from his suffering to reduce and finally eliminate its cause. The Buddha taught four Noble Truths: (a) the omnipresence of suffering; (b) its cause, wrongly directed desire; (c) its cure, the removal of the cause; and (d) the Noble Eightfold Path of self-development which leads to the end of suffering.

7. The eightfold Path consists in Right (or perfect) Views or preliminary understanding. Right Aims or Motive, Right Speech, Right Acts, Right Livelihood, Right Effort, Right Concentration or mind-development, and, finally, Right Samadhi, leading to full enlightenment. As Buddhism is a way of living, not merely a theory of life, the treading of the path is essential to self deliverance. "Cease to do evil, learn to do good, cleanse your own heart; this is the Teaching of the Buddha!"

8. Reality is indescribable, and a God with attributes is not

the Final Reality, but the Buddha, a human being, became the All-Enlightened One, and the purpose of life is the attainment of Enlightenment. This state of consciousness, Nirvana, the extinction of the limitation of selfhood, is attainable on earth. All men and all other forms of life which contain the potentiality of Enlightenment, and the process therefore consists in becoming what you are, "Look within: thou art Buddha."

9. From potential to actual enlightenment there lies the Middle Way, the Eightfold Path "from desire to peace," a process of self-development between the "opposites," avoiding all extremes. The Buddha trod this way to the end, and the only faith required in Buddhism is the reasonable belief that where a Guide has trodden it is worth our while to tread. The Way must be trodden by the whole man, not merely the best of him, and the heart and mind must be developed equally. The Buddha was the All-Compassionate as well as the All-Enlightened One.

10. Buddhism lays great stress on the need of inward concentration and meditation, which leads in time to the development of the inner spiritual faculties. The subjective life is as important as the daily round and periods of quietude for inner activity are essential for a balanced life. The Buddhist should at all times be "mindful and self-possessed," refraining from mental and emotional attachment to "the passing show." This increasingly watchful attitude to circumstances which he knows to be his own creation, helps him to keep his reaction to it always under control.

11. The Buddha said, "Work out your own salvation with diligence." Buddhism knows no authority for truth save the intuition of the individual, and that is authority for himself alone. Each man suffers the consequences of his own acts, and learns thereby, while helping his fellow men to the same deliverance; nor will prayer to the Buddha or to any God prevent an effect from following its cause. Buddhist monks are teachers and exemplars, and in no sense intermediates between Reality and the individual. The utmost tolerance is practiced towards all other religions and philosophies, for no

man has the right to interfere in his neighbor's journey to the Goal.

12. Buddhism is neither pessimistic nor "escapist," nor does it deny the existence of God or soul, though it places its own meaning on these terms. It is, on the contrary, a system of thought, a religion, a spiritual science and a way of life which is reasonable, practical and all-embracing. For over two thousand years it has satisfied the spiritual needs of nearly one third of mankind. It appeals to the West because it has no dogmas, satisfies the reason and the heart alike, insists on self-reliance coupled with tolerance for other points of view, embraces science, religion, philosophy, psychology, ethics and art, and points to man alone as the creator of this present life and sole designer of his destiny.

CHAPTER 6

JUDAISM

Judaism is the religion of the Jews, a tribe of people who came from northern deserts of Arabia to Palestine. There was a long line of Jewish prophets, whose scripture is shared by Judaism and Christianity, and which is the basis for sections of the Koran. In Judaism, the outstanding feature is monotheism and the character of God is personal in many aspects. The Will of God is given supreme importance and the role of man is that of carrying out God's will on earth. A personal relationship was believed to develop between God and the Jews, his "chosen people." The history of the Jews is frequently recounted or referred to in the scriptures. Above all, there is evident persistence of faith in spite of adversity, which has been a feature of Judaism up to the present time, and which clearly contributed to survival when this seemed an impossibility. Interwoven in the history of the Jews are episodes of suffering, which are hard to understand, in a people "chosen by God." The philosophy of learning from suffering is particularly well developed in Jewish scripture. The belief in a Messianic redeemer, who is to "save" the Jewish people, had been interpreted in a political sense in contrast with the Christian belief, which is primarily spiritual. The hope for a human redeemer detracts from the spirituality and religious purity of Judaism.

Morality and monotheism developed in association, in Judaism. In polytheism, the variety of gods had been associated with variability in desires and standards, as in man. In monotheism the "one" God could have only one view on right and wrong, and the unity of authority implied absence of disunity, division or resulting conflict in authority. The centralization of worship at the Temple in Jerusalem (built by Solomon) was an important factor in delimiting worship in smaller centers with inherent variation. The concept of monotheism was developed further by Abraham and Moses, and finds voice particularly in Judasim and Islam at the present time. It may be said to be unacceptable to science, in whose terminology the number "one" is unsuitable, by definition and implicit limitation (and the words "infinite" or "Absolute" suitable).

The concept of God became personalized as Yahweh or Lord, who was considered King of Israel. "He" was the spiritual guide, leader and protector of the Jewish people, and helped them in their flight from the tyranny of Pharaoh, in Egypt, and in their quest for Israel, the "promised land" deigned for their occupancy after many centuries of wandering in Northern Arabia and neighboring lands. The concept of a special relation between God and the Jews has, however, survived, in spite of the repeated sufferings of the Jewish people. Science, however, could hardly countenance a partisan role for God, who created all races.

There developed in Judaism a "moral understanding" of God, concepts of sacrifice and worship, reward and punishment, mercy and love, God's will and human "personal" aspects including hate, anger and jealousy. The latter is particularly difficult in a scientific context, and was replaced by universality of love in Christian Gospels.

Expanding knowledge led to increased personalization of Yahweh, until He came to have many qualities which are normally consideted human. A psychological basis may exist for this formulation — the limitation of knowledge in early civilization may have contributed to the personalization which increased as time passed.

The doctrine of repentance for sins was an inherent part of the teaching of prophets, which included criticism, warning, and admonishment concerning good living and "obedience to God's will." Excessive reliance on sacrifice and ceremony as an appeasement was frowned on by many of them — an attitude reminiscent of that of the Buddha, in relation to Hinduism. The general content of prophetic announcements is repeated by Jesus, whose doctrine of universality of love and forgiveness, as well as personal perfection and sacrifice do not seem to have even an approximate parallel, in Judaism — or in any religion, for that matter.

The importance of the law, written in the Torah, and expanded by experience and tradition, should be realized in assessment of Judaism. Law was considered of divine origin, embodying the Will of God, and obedience to it merited divine award, in this world or the next. The scribes discussed, interpreted and taught the law — in temples, synagogues and later, schools. Accumulated tradition led to a considerable mass of precepts, and adherence to them, as well as knowledge of the Torah, became the ambition of individual Jews. In the context of the present book politics is considered as being separate from spirituality, and regulations are not being dealt with considering their human origin.

The priests were responsible for sacrifice in the temple at Jerusalem. These comprised an offering of a yearling lamb, morning and evening, with accompanied ceremony including meals and drink offerings. Support for the priest and temple involved levies and voluntary contributions.

Expectation of a Messiah was, and still is, a feature of Judaism. The one expected was believed to be a political figure who would be concerned with material affairs and with the welfare of the Jews in this life — rather than the next. In prophetic writings the Messiah was referred to as "Son of Man," "Son of David" and "King of Israel." Signs and omens were expected to precede his coming, including darkening of the sun and moon. The prophet Elijah would also return, before the Messiah.

A period of conflict is expected to precede the coming of the Messiah and this coming is to be preceded by a "spiritual age," the "Kingdom of Heaven" characterized by peace, love, truth, justice and spirituality. A general resurrection and day of judgment are also expected to succeed the final age of tranquillity.

The expectation of a "Messiah" was a hope related to the kingdom of Israel and its restoration. A suffering Messiah was not expected by the Jews. Christ did not fill the role visualized by Jews. The idea, however, as well as the Jewish religion, formed the basis for Christianity, and both Judaism and Christianity formed the basis for Islam. It might be more appropriate, however, to summarize the latter as a rejection of the main principles of Christianity, and a reversion to the Old Testament, perhaps more suited to the Arabs and their way of life.

It is now clear that in Judaism there was an evolution of knowledge of God. The sacrificial ceremonies formed a symbol of gratitude for divine creation and provision for human needs; monotheism contributed to centralization of worship and to acceptance of a concept of authority; association of God with morality followed the acceptance of the idea of "one God." The incompatibility, in science, of accepting that there is a numerical "one" God in view of God's infinity is obvious to those who use mathematics rather than scripture. Only by rationality can man finally mature, agree on unity and infinity of God and reject the old "one God" concept. Science advances knowledge without prejudice. In time all religions will hopefully follow suit.

Expectation of a political Messiah in Judaism contrasts with a spiritual hope in Christianity. The history of the Jewish nation has traditionally involved a personal relationship between God and the Jews. The Jewish faith deals with this world rather than the next; it may be said to be political rather than religious. By contrast Christianity is spiritual in its aspirations,

110

rather than political, and a "spirit of God" in a human being (the "son of Man") fulfilled expectations of a Messiah for some Jews and many Gentiles. Perhaps unity between Judaism and other religions may be conceived in hope and faith in a "Kingdom of Heaven" to come, on earth (as well as in heaven). Such a hope is shared by Christianity, whose principles are based on love, peace and forgiveness of one's enemies. Hinduism shares the love and peace in its teaching and aspirations.

Imperfection is the key to human politics as well as to human self-consciousness, selfishness and resulting egotistical behavior. Any value or issue which savors of primarily human activity exhibits imperfection. This is clearly true of politics, as evidenced by history. Everywhere there has been manifest the egotistical qualities of power-seeking and self-interest. Human history is permeated with the results of human inadequacy — of human imperfection. As long as there is politics inherent in a "religion" such as Judaism, or Islam, there will remain the human retribution and resulting suffering which is part of purely human nature. Only spirituality can exhibit perfection and offer the possibility to man of reaching it.

Separation of politics from religion, in national and international concepts, is essential for an understanding of spirituality and perfection. Man cannot reach beyond himself to supernatural levels by human regulations, philosophy or ideology. A level must be aimed at to be reachable. A level of perfection in man can only be attained if this is aimed at. This requires a supernatural goal, not a political or human one; this only leads to human imperfection.

The development of religion can be compared with the development of science; it has been progressive. This is not to say that a detailed evolution of knowledge can be inferred from the scriptures. It cannot. However, if Judaism and Christianity are considered as one there is a natural and progressive development. The basic supernatural universality of love and education of forgiveness to enemies. In Islam a reversion to primitive attitude is evident, a reflection, perhaps, of the civilizing principles of Christianity.

111

The Christian belief in "original sin," implying human imperfection, is not shared by Judaism, in spite of common scripture in Genesis. The political and material content of faith, in Judaism, extends to legislation in the Torah. In this aspect Judaism is similar to Islam; both of these religions have strong material aspects, and extensive legal systems. There is a corresponding limitation of personal freedom or "free will" and non-acceptance of "original sin."

Monotheism is a feature of Judaism, and in this it long preceded Islam. The idea of one God has many adherents and few realize the important differences between the statements "There is one God" and "God is One." The "One God," if it implies a number, is limiting, according to science. One (in number) and Infinite are different; a scientist would accept that "God is one" or "infinite." The number "one" would not be deemed appropriate, however, by science, to God.

In practically all religions there is a tendency to conceive of God in relation to a particular people. The inherent self-consciousness of man has extended to human societies, communities, races and nationalities. The principle of survival has operated towards self-interest and selfishness. It has caused much of human suffering, aggression and ill-feeling. The conviction of political ideals and of group beliefs, insofar as they are singular and exclusive, tends to discourage tolerance and understanding. The self-conscious character of man has evolved a human concept of a God who is interested in him and in his people. Materialist, and particularly Western, societies have been associated with monotheism and positivity, in relationship between God and man. This association has diminished in the Christian message where self-sacrifice replaces and counters the Old Testament introspective mentality. Central to all religions is the theme of mentality, at the level of the individual, the group, the race, of color, political party and rationality. The evolution of human extrovert thought, compassion and understanding cannot be based on an introspective foundation. Communication on a world scale, with associated education and understanding are a necessary corollary to the development of world understanding. The hitherto selfish character of man must be replaced by un-selfishness. Universal abolition of self-interest is a prerequisite to human cooperation in abolishment of suffering and establishment of universal peace. The coincidence of ultimate human objectives must be universally understood if their unity is to be achieved. Education, without any particular national or religious character, must be broad, even worldwide, to succeed. The interpolation of a conceptual basis for religious change formulated by alteration in human mentality — in this section on Judaism — is not entirely coincidental. The ultimate aim of Judaism is, in fact, spirituality and perfection, in common with Christianity and with Hinduism. In the meantime, however, there is still belief in a forthcoming personal, human Messiah. In common with other religions, however, there is a problem of isolationism in Judaism. Perhaps there is a greater justification for this in Judaism than in other religions, considering historical aspects. The ultimate objective of Judaism, being perfection, is certainly compatible in principle with biology, as a material counterpart. Consideration of Jewish scripture does not detract from the importance of this principle and ultimate objective.

In common with many other religions, Judaism personalized God, in His character, achievements, purpose and decisions. He is believed by Jews to have taken a special interest in them and their welfare; to have guided them eventually to Palestine, the "promised land," following an eventful history. The scriptures provide historical as well as religious information on early Judaism, the people, prophets, beliefs and culture.

The main features of God, in Judaism, as in other religions, have a human character. The distinguishing feature, however, of divine character is infinity, whereas in man abilities and characters are limited. God is said to be omnipotent — there being no limit to His power; omnipresent, in all places; omniscient or all-knowing, and infinite in other ways. However, there is an emphasis on one God (in number) and this, in itself is human and limiting.

Righteousness is the main character of the "One God" of the Jews — Yahweh. Direction of human behavior, guidance and

113

encouragement are important aspects of God in Judaism. Morality in Divinity formed a contrast to the morality of Greek and other Mediterranian gods. Direction centered in "One God" offered a distinct advantage over competing "deities" of former or other religions. Only in Islam does one find similar emphasis on Monotheism. In both Judaism and Islam the authority of "one God" extends to regulations for many aspects of human behavior. The non-acceptance of Christian "original sin," which is based directly on "free will," is consistent with extreme authority and even predestination in Judaism and in Islam. The actuality of free will in the Christian and Western societies is seen to be compatible with the advisory role of authority and the disassociation of religion and politics. Where this principle is carried to extremes, however, in individual interpretation of scripture and in personal conscience, the absence of authority leads to excessive "freedom" and return to selfish patterns of human behavior.

Prophets were people who were believed to speak to the people on behalf of God. The English word prophet is derived from the Greek **prophetes**, literally "to speak for." A prophet was considered to be (particularly) receptive to God's will, so that he was "inspired" and the will of God was "revealed" to him. The Greek meaning is similar to that in Hebrew.

A series of prophets appeared in Judaism (Christianity and Islam) who were generally holy and righteous people. They voiced justice, promoted what they believed to be the will of Yahweh, the Lord, or "Spirit of God." The writings of some are preserved in the Old Testament.

The spirit of God was believed, as in Christianity, to be of God and from God, and to be God. In Islam the spirit of God was sent from God (in space, as it were) and is considered separate from God. The concept as in Islam is of a distant, single, distinct and separate God. Prophets were believed to act as messengers on God's behalf. Outstanding among them were Abraham, Moses, Elijah, Isaiah, Jeremiah and Moses. Moses was given the ten commandments by the Lord, and saw the spirit of God, in a bush. He heard the voice of Yahweh who spoke to him; many others were also spoken to by the "Lord."

114

The concept of God's chosen people, of a special relation between the Jews and God, is found to some extent in all religions, though, in an historical content, in Judaism and Islam particularly. Any race or people or community, being human and self-conscious (this knowledge of self is the basis of free-will and of Christian "original sin"), is interested in relating to God and in God's relation to itself; similarly in the individual. Thus, for each person God is the "being" which one relates to and vice versa. This relationship forms the foundation for the idea that there is one God, which in scientific terms is false. The truth is that God is infinite. The "one spirit of God" is involved with a race or a prophet, in space and time. The spirit of God is only "part" of the "essence" of God, the Absolute or Infinite. In general, Western religions emphasize their one God, whereas this emphasis is not found in Buddhism or Hinduism. The Gospels, however, do not limit God to "one" in number, but there is a distinction drawn between the Creator (The Universal God, or "Father") and the spirit of God (paraclete or counsellor, appearing as spiritual "son" of God, carrying out the "Father's" will). These are formed of the same essence of perfection, as in Hinduism. Judaism and Islam are the pre- eminently monotheistic religions. Furthermore, in these two religions, believers have faith in God's special relation to them. This is indeed "original sin" or self-awareness carried to a natural egocentric conclusion. Christianity is considered to be saved from this human egocentricity by Jesus (meaning: saver, in Aramaic), metaphorically, psychologically, spiritually and communally. Christianity is open to all, nonracial and extrovert in universal outlook.

A scientific or objective view of monotheistic religions implies that in these God is believed to exist for man's benefit, including intercession in human history. In the spiritual religions, Christianity and Hinduism, man is believed to serve God in becoming united ("one") with him, in meditation and in action. The prevention of suffering, as well as healing, is, par excellence, Christian in principle and practice. The importance of medical science in Western social development is a natural corollary of the Christian outlook.

There is, in the Christian religion and peoples, development of an extrovert or "love your neighbor" character, at an international as well as individual level. From a purely humanitarian or biological view, such principles as underline the change from Old to New Testament reflect those which are associated with "civilization." Practice does not always follow principles, in any religion, and the internecine strife associated nowadays with Islam has, until recently, been shared by Christians.

Two prominent features of early Judaism were ceremony and morality. Associated with ceremony there was an inherent variation in custom, worship, statues or idols, and prayer. A particular feature of development in Judaism was the abolishment of "idols" with an emphasis on "unity" and on "one" God. The basis for this trend was in the teaching of Abraham and of Moses. The basic initial implication of monotheism was a denial of "more Gods than one." However, as in Islam, the "one God" idea has essentially survived. With the advent of modern science and its use as a parameter for scripture, the substitution of "infinite" or "absolute" is logical. How the professedly monotheistic religions survive will depend on the degree of international and particularly racial communication and admixture, and on knowledge of the difference between the numeral "one" and infinity.

The increasing acceptance that man should "follow God's Will" and "keep his commandments" led to an evolution of a multiplicity of regulations which an Orthodox Jew is expected to follow. The letter of the law in regulations concerning behavior is reminiscent of the detail recommended and observed in ceremony, in Jewish and other religions. Much of this is evidently of human political origin, even if generally considered as scriptural, "from God" by inspiration or otherwise. More enlightened or scientific minds tend to admit a human element, in determination of ceremonial and behavioral norms, and regulations in scripture. The paucity of claims of communication of the spoken word by God to man is matched by the lack of scientific credibility of individual claims of personal revelation.

The relation of nationalism to religion has been closer in Judaism — and in some Islamic countries more than others. The relation of spirituality to moral standards is recognized in all religions. The degree to which religion dictates laws is one of the main factors in some totalitarian governments. In general, there is compatibility between all systems of spirituality and political systems. Some primitive customs such as polygamy and retaliative murder (in Islam) are, however, illegal in civilized countries. The existence of human freedom is particularly existent in religions which are non-political, e.g. Hinduism and Christianity. Totalitarianism is especially evident where Governments claim to enact God's laws.

The question of laws ("from God") and obedience relates to "free will" and "disobedience." Judaism and Islam command obedience to "laws of God," whereas Christianity guides, with authority, in perfection, teaching the freedom of will of the individual and his less than human performance. Perfection requires much more than this, if the ideals of the Catholic Christian Church are to be emulated voluntarily — returning one's will to God. Such high ideals are unpopular, because of the spirituality of their nature and their "detachment" from pleasure and materialism.

Religion, like science, has evolved by increase in knowledge and understanding. This evolution is a continuous process, past and present. Revelation was the older process of "revealing God's Will" for man. Reason and, particularly, life science form the modern counterpart of this process. Religion must keep up to date in life science, so that it will have an informed opinion and ability to advise morally. The continuation of the evolution of religious knowledge, understanding and teaching is essential while imperfection remains. This shall be for the duration of existence of the human nature of man. Only a totality of knowledge leads to completeness of understanding and of compassion. Thus only spirituality, not materialism, can be sufficient as man's aim.

It can never be claimed, with proof and finality, that any prophet is the last to whom the will of God is revealed. While man is human there are limitations in his character. His finiteness engenders imperfection.

Man will always require guidance, since he is imperfect, and disobedient in nature to God in having free will. The incompleteness of human knowledge requires an increase in human advance in knowledge for all time. There is no end except the end of human nature and the transition to divine. Thus there was no one human who imparted to man all knowledge. We can only learn by "building on experience," and in stages, from what we know before. There is not a single or complete step to completeness of knowledge. Only spirituality can possess the qualities that are supernatural, infinite and divine. No scripture has been a complete or final revelation. The evolution, the revelation, the increase in knowledge must continue until the final phase of spirituality. In the meantime there is required a detachment from materialism and a realization of the universal imperfection of human nature.

The laws of scripture and of nations have developed because of man's imperfection. Laws are not required for perfection of actions based on spirituality. Laws are political, not spiritual. Their necessity, based on imperfection, their variation according to nation, race and culture, is related to religion insofar as religion is political. Politics can only have a limited platform in man's improvement. Perfection requires more than this. It implies universality, the supernatural, the infinite. Politics is for outward behavior, for humanitarian and limited purposes. When it competes with religion it wins on material ground and loses on objectives and methods, though, generally speaking, the betterment and the future of man are the common aim. Human laws and values are lacking in divine nature, perfection and spirituality. "Divine" laws are merely a guidance to an ideal which is perfection of spirituality, of mentality or cosmic consciousness. Detailed legislation militates against the freedom of man. It may be considered a phase in evolution to becoming the informed, educated, understanding, intelligent, compassionate, forgiving human being. Wisdom is a feature of knowledge and obliterates the need for legal fetters. Regulations are to protect man against primitive

118

and barbarous instincts and qualities that were the basis for cannibalism, polygamy, infanticide, "reciprocity of diplomacy" (a "slave for a slave," etc.), and stoning to death.

It is not intended that these features of political and legal aspects of "religion" be considered solely to relate to Judaism. They are found in Islam also. The concepts of law and proper behavior should be understood in the context of suitable motivation — for perfection. Such motivation should be based on education, knowledge, understanding and compassion, as in medicine — and, uniquely among religions, in the principles of Christianity.

Scriptures may "date" a religion and limit its proper development. Excessive reliance on, and adherence to, a scripture will, in time, lead to antiquarian character. Evolution and expansion of teaching and doctrines is a natural corollary to religious survival and biological significance. The need for authority (rather than individual decisions) is based on the superiority of collective over singular human thought, consideration and judgement.

Principles and concepts are visible; they are adaptible, have universal applicability and stand the test of time. Love for God and our neighbor is an example of a concept that will not easily become outmoded. Laws are human in nature, content and relevance. They aim to protect the individual and society. They serve to further self-interest, materialism, personal and community economics. Imperfection is the character of man which necessitates laws. The existence of laws supports man's imperfection. Perfection would not require them. The "Kingdom of Heaven" or "End of Days," with a universality of benevolence, by all towards all, will, hopefully, end the need for laws, human or "God-given."

The divine origin of laws is questionable, except, perhaps, for divine inspiration as a contributory factor in their formation; from a scientific viewpoint the human factor in retaliative or recriminatory laws — their content of "spitefulness" — is clearly human rather than divine. The finiteness (or limitation) of human love and forgiveness which characterizes human legislation is characteristically human.

The infinity of God's love, and absence of limitation, can not be the basis for "reciprocity of action" ("an eye for an eye," etc.). There is clearly a human contribution, even if scripture is claimed to be entirely divine in origin.

An evolution of reason and understanding is present in Judaic scriptures. The unwinding of a mental image of God is accompanied by a process of "civilization" which should logically culminate in principles of Christian love, forgiveness, compassion and healing. There is a trend away from material things, and towards spiritual, from Judaism to Christianity taken in continuity. On its own, the religion of Judaism has been said to be material and political in nature — as in Islam. The ideal of spiritual perfection is "grounded" or tied firmly to earthly values and levels by political and legal content — in Judaism and its close relation, Islam. It is in the nature of man to be averse to spirituality, to perfection as an ideal and thus to Christian principles.

The unity of all thought, effort and compassion, the extroversion of an introverted mentality, the extension of love to all mankind including one's enemies, a logical approach to suffering, a recognition of the centrality of human imperfection in its causation, the ultimate in self-sacrifice, above all the infusion of spirituality into human life — these are natural goals of religion based on perfect ideals. Taking perfection as the real motive of human life, one does not find it in a religion allied to human values and to politics. Taking objectives into account, spirituality as a feature, and considering perfection as an ideal, the continued guidance of the Holy Spirit — Hinduism and Christianity — especially Roman Catholicism — emerge as religions par excellence, with the stipulation that there are necessary features of a religion absent in the former but present in the latter.

Judaism emerges in scientific perspective like Islam, as a primitive religion, particularly because of its inherent self-righteousness and presumption reflected in a nationalistic and introverted mentality. The features of Islam that come to mind are similar except that they pertain to the exclusiveness and finality in prophecy of a prophet, a reciprocal prescription for murder, retention of severance of a limb and stoning to death, polygamy and castigation by vague and ignorant inference of the principles of Christian faith, which alone offer a philosophy fit to lead to universal human love and spirituality.

It is not proposed to detail Jewish law. From a scientific or objective standpoint laws or politics are not primarily a part of religion. Religion is confined to spirituality, in the context of the present approach. The things that are Caesar's are being left to his successors. It is clear that politics and religion do not mix, the former dealing with the essence of perfection, the latter with human finite, material values. History has borne out the principle that divergence or variation in ideals, culture, language, and religion leads to conflict.

The cessation of cultural development in the Middle East, particularly among Arab peoples following an initial growth, can probably be attributed to the belief that a scripture represented the ultimate in God's revelation. In science there is no forseeable final stage in revelation of knowledge. Revelation of ideas is a common occurrence among scientists and it is more likely to occur from a divine source than purely from man.

Consciousness, mentality, mental attitude — whatever we understand by the evolution of a civilized human mind, may have evolved to a final level in Christ, the complete answer, as it were, to suffering, to man's inhumanity. For the Jews this did not seem to provide the answer. Is there a possibility of improvement of human behavior and attitude beyond that which is Christian, in principle? Its will for man — prevention of suffering, healing, giving, love and forgiveness? Or is the future a political one, involved in aggression, human and always imperfect? The character of man is fraught with differences, selfishness, imperfection and the independence of mind that means turning away from God. The only perfection is spirituality.

CHAPTER 7

ISLAM AND "ONE GOD"

Islam is an "Old Testament" religion, emphasizing "One God" or Allah, "The God." The scripture is the Koran and this includes laws prescribing a way of life which is primarily Arabic. Moslems are expected to pray five times daily, to fast for one month a year (Ramadhan), to give alms to the poor, and to visit Mecca for a pilgrimage (Haj) once in their lifetime. There is a common basis in early Western scriptures between Judaism, Christianity and Islam. Judaism and Islam are similar in principles, though having different scriptures. Islam can be considered to be compatible with Christianity or to con- tradict it, depending on interpretation.

Members of Islam are called Moslems. The name Moslem means follower of God and as such implies obedience to God, and perfection. This contrasts with other religions which ad- mit imperfection of man; especially Christianity, with its doc- trine of "Original sin," which implies disobedience (the op- posite to Moslem obedience), free will and imperfection due to this freedom, and associated independence of God's will. In

Islam, however, there are laws governing punishment for human misbehavior, and the existence of such laws (in the Koran) for mankind implies imperfection. There is, further, the problem of free will versus predestination in Islam, which are incompatible with one another. A question central to Life Science and Religion is, "Is man perfect?" Biologically speaking, man is imperfect. Spiritually and morally man is imperfect also. Imperfection appears biologically to characterize not alone Christians but members of all religions. It is implied in the Koran that Mary was without sin, and thus perfect. In Christianity she is an immaculate conception, born without original sin and according to tradition, giving birth to Christ without distress in labor — the result of original sin in Eve and other women. This implies that she always obeyed God's will, and was not "disobedient" like the rest of mankind.

Islam is a religion and a way of life. It is based on the Koran, the scripture whose contents are considered to have been revealed to Muhammed between 600 A.D. and 650 A.D. Islam means submission and obedience to the Will of God. Members of Islam are sometimes called Muhammedans, since in becoming a Muslim one says, "There is one God who is Allah and Muhammed is his prophet." The term Muhammedan, however, is considered unsuitable by Moslems in spite of the requirement of accepting Muhammed as above the other prophets, by implication. The word Islam is derived from Salam which means peace. The way of life which Islam prescribes is claimed to operate towards peace in the future of man. The proposal is that if man does all things in obedience to God's will there will result perfect harmony in human life and relationships. The word peace is considered to mean not alone absence of war and fighting, but harmony in relations among men and also peace of mind which is associated with contentment and satisfaction in carrying out actions according to the overall plan of God. The meaning of Islam implies that man obeys God and Moslems are perfect people whose lives are lived in obedience to God's desires. However, retaliation is condoned in the Koran ("A slave for a slave," etc.), though

124

forgiveness is stated to be more acceptable to "the God." This is in contrast with Christianity, which accepts free will, human imperfection and absence of human obedience to God's will.

The Koran

III. 144. "Muhammed is not more than an Apostle: many were the Apostles that passed away before him."

XVIII. 110. "Say I am but a man like yourselves (but) the inspiration has come to me, that your God is one God: whoever expects to meet the Lord, let him work righteousness, and, in the worship of his Lord, admit no one as partner."

Moslems, however, consider Muhammed above the other prophets since he is claimed to be the final prophet or the "Seal of the prophets."

XXXIII. 40. "Muhammed is not the father of any of your men, but (he is) the Apostle of God, and the Seal of the prophets; and God has full knowledge of all things."

The Koran is claimed to be an "inspiration" indirectly from God, through the Angel Gabriel, who appeared, "in the distance," to Muhammed.

LIII. 1-18. "By the star when it goes down, your companion is neither astray nor being misled. Nor does he say (aught) of (his own) desire. It is no less than inspiration sent down to him; he was taught by one mighty in power. Endued with wisdom; for he appeared (in stately form) while he was in the highest part of the horizon; then he approached and came closer, and was at a distance of but two bow-lengths or (even) nearer; so did (God) to convey the inspiration to His servant — (conveyed) what He (meant) to convey."

It will be noticed that the angel Gabriel is not named; also, God is not mentioned as the source of revelation.

LXIII. 1-18. "The (Prophet's) (mind and) heart in no way falsified that which he saw, will ye then dispute with him concerning what he saw? For indeed he saw him at a second descent, near the Lote-tree beyond which none may pass; near it is the Garden of abode; behold, the Lote-tree was shrouded (in mystery unspeakable) (his) sight never swerved, nor did it go wrong for truly did he see of the signs of his Lord, the greatest."

"Signs of his Lord" is vague as evidence concerning the origin of the Koran.

XLVIII. 10. "Verily those who plight their fealty to thee do no less than plight their fealty to God..."

The following extract is claimed to be on St. John's Gospel.

LXI. 6. "And remember, Jesus, the son of Mary, said: 'O children of Israel, I am the apostle of God (sent) to you, confirming the law (which came) before me, and giving glad tidings of an apostle to come after me. Whose name shall be Ahmed.' "

Ahmed, however, is a mistranslation.

The Holy Spirit, which is a personification of God in time and space, is foretold in St. John's Gospel, according to Christianity, and appeared to the Apostles. The Greek word (St. John XIV: 16, XV: 26, and XVI: 7) in John is paraclete, which means advocate, not comforter or merciful one. The word Ahmed in the Koran is claimed by Moslems to derive from Periclytos and it is claimed that there is a corruption of St. John's text, from paracletos to periclytos. In Christianity the Paraclete is the Holy Spirit of God, which is man's advocate or guide and which appeared on a number of occasions (in time and space) to guide the church and to help men to know the right path. The same role is understood for the Holy Spirit of God in the Gita, which compares remarkably, in the relevant section (IV, 6,7,8), with the extracts in John.

VII. 157. "Those who follow the Apostle, the unlettered Prophet, whom they find mentioned in their own (Scriptures), in the law and the gospel;..."

This verse states that Muhammed was mentioned in the Gospel. There is no such mention in the four gospels accepted by Christians as the main basis of Christianity. The immediately previous note, on Paraclete, applies here. The role of the Holy Spirit of God, which is the Universal Spirit of God, which is God, is being attributed to Muhammed. The Holy Spirit of

God has appeared, as foretold in St. John's Gospel, on a number of occasions, to the apostles, and in the Old Testament.

The following note indicates that the instruction of Islam is for the unlettered or primitive people.

LXII. 2. "It is He who has sent amongst the unlettered an apostle from among themselves to rehearse to them His signs, to sanctify them, and to instruct them in scripture and wisdom — although they had been, before, in manifest error..."

II. 151. "A similar (favor have ye already received) in that we have sent among you an Apostle of your own, rehearsing to you our signs, and sanctifying you, and instructing you in scripture and wisdom. And in new knowledge."

LXXXI. 22-25. "And (O people) your companion is not one possessed; and without doubt he saw him in the clear horizon. Neither doth he withhold grudgingly a knowledge of the unseen. Nor is it the word of an evil spirit accursed."

Presumably the vision of Muhammed refers to the angel Gabriel — it is not made clear, however, who he claimed to see.

The Koran is believed by Moslems to be the word of "the God" (Il Allah). God is considered to have composed the Koran hundreds of thousands of years before it was communicated to Muhammed. The Koran is believed to have been communicated in Arabic to the angel Gabriel. He, in turn, is said to have spoken its contents to Muhammed from 610 A.D. God is not considered to have talked to Gabriel but to have communicated with him in an unknown manner, in Arabic. Muhammed was "inspired" with the various suras (verses) of the Koran in a series of meditations, which he practiced. It was his custom to visit a cave at Mount Hijra and to roll himself in a blanket and lie prostrate. His meditation was a voluntary process and he practiced this over many years. The revelations which he received are considered by Muslims to be authentically the word of God. After Muhammed's death they were written at various times on leaves, bone, parchment, and papyri which were hidden in different places and later put together in an order avowedly determined by the prophet Muhammed. This order was not chronological, as evidenced by reference to historical occurrences at about this time.

The Koran is a collection of writings on different subjects and one should have an open mind in attempting to understand its contents. Most people would expect some sequence in such a book — there is none. Also there are many apparent contradictions. Islam is stated to be close to Christianity, yet all the basic tenets of Christianity appear to be denied. There are different attitudes towards Jews and Christians. There are various instructions about alcohol consumption. There are many extracts which are similar to sections in the Jewish Torah or have striking resemblance to Christian scriptures. It has been implied that, from the aspect of life science, the Koran may be considered a "private revelation" since it was only to one person. Claims have also been made that Islam forms a heresy in the Christian sense, denying practically all the fundamental beliefs of Christianity; original sin, divine nature or "sonship" of Christ, the "trinity," healing by the "spirit of God" in Christ, redemption by Christ and his crucifixion and death on the Cross. The harsh laws of Islam contrast with the forgiveness of Christ. The monogamy and bias against divorce which is in Christianity contrasts with permitted polygamy and (scriptural) ease of divorce in Islam. There is no claim of physical healing by Muhammed, and no emphasis on a policy of prevention of human suffering.

The Koran is composed of suras or verses. They are not arranged in a chronological order but in the order of their length, the longest being at the beginning (with one exception). The topics vary considerably and include laws, directions for marriage and divorce, qualities of God, description of heaven and hell, "signs" or proofs that God exists, directions for inheritance, comments on Christians and Jews and their beliefs. It also refers to Muhammed's personal exploits and private life. There is no sequence or logical arrangement in the Koran. It is claimed that the book is unique because it is the word of God. Its vagueness and statements without explana-

128

tion as well as changes of verses are said be justified because all things are possible for God.

XIII. 39. "God doth blot out or confirm what he pleaseth; with Him is the Mother of the Book."

From the scientific viewpoint the changing of scriptures cannot be a function of God, since He is generally conceived as eternal and unchanging.

Many features of the Koran indicate that it is a reversion of or turning back from Christianity to the Old Testament. It has been suggested that it contains extracts of Jewish and Christian traditions and stories. It is in part historical and includes events and customs of tribes of Arabia. The emphasis is on one God, distant, all-powerful, merciful, having ability to create man in a moment of time and predestining human history and behavioral patterns. Thus, God made each individual either good or evil and promoted heavenly bliss for the good and eternal fire for the evil. Predestination is a feature of Islam which is inherent in the Koran being composed long before events described. There is a problem about reconciling the early composition of the Koran by God with subsequent human freedom of choice. If God knew beforehand all that would take place then it appears that man had or has no choice in behavior. Nowadays, an attempt is being made to introduce free will as a concept into interpretations of the Koran. It is implied that when man becomes good or evil he is making a choice. However, if potential for evil exists in all mankind, this is virtually the same as the Christian teaching of original sin.

The Koran is accepted emotionally by Moslems, without question. Western society uses reason more than emotion in evaluation of scripture as well as of science. It is inevitable that a rational approach be made to the Koran in examination of its relation to life science. Where a scripture does not appear to be compatible with rational concepts then it is to be expected that it will be replaced by scientific and humanitarian values. Understanding of this requirement can be expected to relate initially only to those who are sufficiently educated. Unreasoning acceptance of a scripture does not usually occur in Western society because of education and associated rationality. Understanding is increased due to scientific advances. The spread of knowledge and truth can be expected to parallel education, and belief which does not stand up to critical scientific evaluation will persist only among the uneducated.

The following are extracts from the (translated) Koran with comments. The meaning of "allegorical" from the first sura quoted here is "to be understood symbolically." It is not made clear which suras are basic and which are allegorical.

III. 7. "He it is who has sent down to thee the book, in it are verses basic or fundamental (of established meaning): They are the foundation of the book; others are allegorical. But those in whose hearts is a perversity follow the part thereof that is allegorical, seeking discord, and searching for its hidden meanings, but no one knows its hidden meanings except God. And those who are firmly grounded in knowledge say, 'We believe in the book: the whole of it is from our Lord,' and none will grasp the Message except men of understanding."

The confirmatory nature of the Koran is referred to, and the implication is made that the Koran is not a new doctrine. This contrasts with Christianity, which introduced new principles of infinite love, peace and forgiveness.

XLI. 43. "Nothing is said to thee that was not said to the apostles before thee; that thy Lord has at His command (all) forgiveness as well as a most grievous penalty."

XVII. 106. "(It is) a Koran which we have divided (into parts from time to time), in order that thou mightest recite it to man at intervals; we have revealed it by stages."

Changes in the Koran have been estimated to number about 200. Most religions could not accept changes as acceptable in a scripture, or as indicative of an origin from God, who is unchanging.

XV. 101, 102. "When we substitute one revelation for another — and God knows best what He reveals (in stages) — they say, 'Thou art but a forger.' But most of them understand not. Say, the Holy Spirit has brought the revelation from thy Lord in Truth, in order to strengthen those who believe, and as a guide and glad tidings to Muslims."

Discrepancy is most apparent in attitude to Christianity, implied confirmation being in complete contrast to Islamic denial of all the basic Christian concepts:

IV. 82. "Do they not consider the Koran (with care)? Had it been from other than God, they would surely have found therein much discrepancy."

X. 37. "This Koran is not such as can be produced by other than God; on the contrary it is a confirmation of (revelations) that went before it, and a fuller explanation of the Book — wherein there is no doubt — from the Lord of the Worlds."

It is clear that the apostle Muhammed was sent to teach the Arab people only from the following verse:

X. 47. "To every people (was sent) an Apostle: when their Apostle comes (before them), the matter will be judged between them and with justice, and they will not be wronged."

The idea of one indivisible God is considered incompatible with God having a "son." In Christianity the "sonship" of Christ simply means that the "spirit of God" (which is God) was in Christ, not separate from him.

XV. 110. "Say 'Praise be to God,' who begets no son and has no partner in (His) dominion — nor (needs) He any to protect Him from humiliation: yes, magnify Him for His greatness and glory."

It is stated that "Apostles" had wives and children. Christ is thus an exception — or not an apostle. In Christianity the spirit of Christ was of and from God, and he is considered (spiritually) the "son" of God (not physically).

XIII. 38. "We did send apostles before thee, and appointed for them wives and children; and it was never the part of an apostle to bring a sign except as God permitted (or commanded). For each period is a book (revealed)."

The "things in which they differ" included the divine spiritual sonship of Christ, the trinity, the death of Christ, and all the fundamentals of Christianity.

XVI. 64. "And we sent down the book to thee for the express purpose that thou should make clear to them those things in which they differ, and that it should be a guide and a mercy to those who believe."

The sign or proofs of the existence of God are suited to primitive or unlettered people. A modern counterpart would involve the whole content of life sciences, with special emphasis on the mental development of man.

XVI. 65. "And verily in cattle (too) will ye find an instructive sign, from what is within their bodies between excretions and blood, we produce, for your drink, milk, pure and agreeable to those who drink it."

The unity which should exist in religion can only be understood in terms of the universal imperfection of man in finite qualities and reproductive pattern. This is the Original Sin of Christianity. The unique perfection of Christ and Mary needs to be understood rather than denied.

XLIII. 13. "The same religion has He established for you as that which He enjoined on Noah — that which we have sent by inspiration to thee — and that which we enjoined on Abraham, Moses, and Jesus: Namely that ye should remain steadfast in religion, and make no divisions therein."

11. 87. "We gave Moses the book and followed him up with a succession of Apostles; we gave Jesus the son of Mary clear (signs) and strengthened him with the Holy Spirit. Is it that whenever there comes to you an Apostle with what ye yourselves desire not, ye are puffed up with pride? Some ye called imposters, and others ye slay."

"We" (meaning God?) "strengthened him with the Holy Spirit" may be taken to highlight the difference between Islam and Christianity. In Islam the Holy Spirit was sent by God and was separate from Him. In Christianity the Holy Spirit (here) means the spirit of God — from God — and is God. The last line implies that apostles were slain; however, the slaying of Christ is denied in the Koran.

Signs

The two important topics "signs" and predestination are referred to in the following two verses. Predestination is referred to in various parts of the Koran, some passages being against it and some in favor.

132

VI. 109. "They swear their strongest oaths by God, that if a (special) sign came to them, by it they would believe. Say: 'Certainly (all) signs are in the power of God; but what will make you (Moslems) realize that (even) if (special) signs came, they will not believe?' Even if we did send unto them angels, and the dead did speak unto them, and we gathered together all things before their very eyes, they are not the ones to believe, unless it is in God's plan. But most of them ignore (the truth)."

The "Signs" or proofs that are quoted in the two verses that follow refer to a she-camel (various stories are told concerning her), night and day, animal life, winds and clouds. These "signs" are reminiscent of early Hindu concepts of God. Biologically they are not comparable to the miracles of healing, in Cairo recently, which are evidence of the divine nature of Mary and Jesus, and thus support Christianity.

XVII. 59. "And we refrain from sending the signs, only because the men of former generations treated them as false; we sent the She-camel to the Thamud to open their eyes, but they treated her wrongfully; we only send the signs by way of terror (and warning from evil)."

XVII. 12. "We have made the night and the day as two (of our) signs: the sign of the night have we obscured, while the sign of the day we have made to enlighten you; that ye may seek bounty from your Lord, and that ye may know the number and count to the years; all things have we explained in detail."

II. 164. "To an earth that is dead; in the beasts all kinds that He scatters through the earth; in the change of the winds, and the clouds which they trail like their slaves between the sky and the earth; (here) indeed are signs for a people that are wise."

LVI. 68-69. "See ye that water which ye drink? Do ye bring it down (in rain) from the cloud or do we?"

Genesis

The story of Adam and Eve is told similarly to (Christian) Genesis, including the "tree of knowledge" and "the Fall" from the Garden of Paradise (state of happiness). The following passage may be taken to support free will, whereas others oppose it.

II. 35. "We said, 'O Adam, dwell thou and thy wife in the Garden; and eat of the bountiful things therein as (where and when) ye will; but approach not this tree, or ye run into harm and transgression.' "

II. 36. "Then did Satan make thou slip from the (Garden), and get them out."

II. 38. "We said, 'Get ye down all from here; and if, as is sure, there comes to you guidance from Me, whosoever follows my guidance, on them shall be no fear, nor shall they grieve.' "

II. 39. "But those who reject Faith and believe our signs, they shall be companions of the Fire; they shall abide therein."

VII. 22. "So by deceit he brought about their fall: when they tasted of the tree their shame became manifest to them, and they began to sew together the leaves of the Garden over their bodies and their Lord called unto them. 'Did I not forbid you that tree, and tell you that Satan was an avowed enemy unto you?' "

VII. 33. "Say: The things that my Lord hath indeed forbidden are: shameful deeds, whether open or secret; sins and trespasses against truth or reason; assigning of partners to God, for which he hath given no authority. And saying things about God of which ye have no knowledge."

The following verse underlines predestination.

VII. 34. "To every people is a term appointed: when their term is reached, not an hour can they cause delay, nor (an hour) can they advance (it in anticipation)."

III. 64. "Say: 'O People of the book come to common terms as between us and you: that we worship none but God; that we associate no partners with him: That we erect not, from among ourselves, Lords and patrons other than God.' If then they turn back say ye, 'Bear witness that we (at least) are Moslems (bowing to God's will).' "

The strict monotheism of Moses is evident here. It is as if God is a single person, one in number rather than infinite. Science would not agree with pure "monotheism," but could accept the implied unity of the statement "God is one." In the

Koran both these claims are made: "There is one God" and "God is one." Only the latter is compatible with the scientific meaning of one. What is being denied is probably that there is a number of gods. However, in science, no number — only infinity — can be applied to God.

IV. 47. "O ye people of the book, believe in what we have (now) revealed, confirming what was (already) with you, before we change the face and fame of some (of you) beyond all recognition, and turn them hindwards, or curse them as we cursed the Sabbath-breakers, for the decision of God must be carried out."

The vicious type of description of God given here is hard to understand. Turning faces or heads back to front is not the sort of activity a scientist associates with God, in spite of the occurrence of some gross birth defects spontaneously in man. Neither is cursing considered an attribute of God in civilized society.

Revelation

IV. 163. "We have sent thee inspiration, as we sent it to Noah and the messengers after him; we sent inspiration to Abraham, Ismail, Isaac, Jacob and the Tribes, to Jesus, Jonah, Aaron, and Solomon, and to David we gave the psalms."

IV. 164. "Of some apostles we have already told thee the story; of others we have not; and to Moses God spoke direct."

God spoke direct only to Moses, according to Islam. This presumably means that Moses was greater than Muhammed. In becoming a Moslem, however, one has to acknowledge Muhammed, not Moses. Obviously if God spoke to Moses he could, though not human, have spoken to Muhammed. It is accepted by all, however, that He did not. In Christianity it was the Holy Spirit of God, that is, God being personified in time and space, who spoke to Moses and gave him the ten commandments and appeared on various occasions.

V. 71. "Say, 'O People of the Book, ye have no ground to stand upon unless ye stand fast by the law, the Gospel, and all the revelation that has come to you from your Lord.' "

The "law" and the "gospel" cannot both be obeyed since they are diametrically opposite concerning killing, adultery, divorce, polygamy, forgiveness, fundamentals of belief and pilgrimage.

There is a party among them on the right course — peculiarly many Moslems consider all Christians as "unbelievers" and claim the Gospels are unacceptable. If some are "on the right course" presumably they have proper scriptures in their gospels. Incidentally, only one gospel is mentioned in the Koran. The existence of four gospels is not mentioned anywhere.

V. 69. "If only they had stood fast by the law, the Gospel, and all the revelation that was sent to them from their Lord, they would have enjoyed Happiness from every side. There is from among them a party on the right course; but many of them follow a course that is evil."

XXIX. 46. "And dispute ye not with the People of the book, except with means better (then mere disputation), unless it be with those of them who inflict wrong (and injury); but say, 'We believe in the revelation which has come down to us and in that which came down to you; Our God and your God is one; and it is to Him we bow (in Islam).' "

The assertion that Christians are Muslims may be reconciled with scripture or not, according to interpretation. One of the main problems in comparative religions is the relation between Islamic and Christian scriptures. On the one hand Islam can be considered an outright rejection of the fundamentals of Christianity; on the other hand the close relation between them is emphasized in the Koran. In the past, politics has often become involved with religion and both ignorance and bigotry have contributed to separation. Attitudes in the Koran, to Christians and Jews, depended on the historical situation at the time, and varied during Muhammed's lifetime. One sign of change in attitude was apparent in the change in direction of prostration, from Jerusalem, to Mecca.

XXVIII. 53. "And when it is recited to them, they say, 'We believe therein, for it is the truth from our Lord. Indeed we have been Muslims (bowing to God's will) from before this.' "

V. 85. "Strongest among men in enmity to the believers wilt thou find the Jews and Pagans; and nearest among them in love to the believers wilt thou find those who say: 'We are Christians,' because amongst these are men devoted to in learning and men who have renounced the world, and they are not arrogant."

V. 86. "And when they listen to the revelation received by the Apostle, thou wilt see their eyes overflowing with tears, for they recognize the truth; they pray, 'Our Lord we believe; write us down among the witnesses.' "

II. 134-136. "They say, 'Become Jews or Christians if ye should be guided (to salvation).' Say thou: 'Nay (I would rather) be the Religion of Abraham the true, and he joined not gods with God.' "

This confirms the Old Testament nature of Islam.

Creation and Evolution

The idea of instantaneous creation is contrary to the theory of creative evolution. In Western society it is generally accepted that evolution is 99% proved. Advances in science are continually supporting creative evolution. Science now accepts that evolution operated in human creation and descriptions of instant creation are accepted only for the time they were written and for people who had no knowledge of modern biology. Biologists consider that some steps in the evolution of man were associated with a change in the number of chromosomes. Recent evidence brings understanding of evolutionary and biological change down to the molecular level and we are far less concerned now than formerly with searching for the "missing link." The whole process of development of biochemical material can be almost completely traced through step-like changes in molecular structure. There are series of amino acids which clearly point to a step-wise evolutionary constructive process. The genes of chimpanzees and of man are 99% the same. Also, in comparative physiology the evolutionary changes of organs such as the kidneys, lungs, alimentary canal, heart, brain, etc. are evident.

137

There appears to be a definite contradiction and incompatibility between life science and instant creation. Life scientists believe God is omnipotent only over a period of time, in biological terms.

However, the instant creation of Adam, meaning "man," is believed in by some.

VII. 189. "It is He who created you from a single person, and made his mate of like nature, in order that he might dwell with her (in love)."

The following accounts of creative evolution bear little resemblance to modern knowledge. A Koran of divine origin would presumably exhibit scientific content much greater than this since God is all-knowing. It was up to date, however, in the 7th Century.

XXII. 5. "Consider that we created you out of dust, then out of sperm, then out of leech-like clot, then out of a morsel of flesh, partly formed."

XXIII. 12-14. "Man we did create from a quintessence (of clay); then we placed him as (a drop of) sperm in a place of rest, firmly fixed; then we made the sperm into a clot of congealed blood; then of that clot we made a lump; then we made out of that lump bones and clothed the bones with flesh; then we developed out of it another creature. So blessed be God, the best to create."

XL. 67. "It is He who has created you from dust, then from a sperm-drop, then from a leech-like clot."

LXXXII. "He who created thee, fashioned thee in due proportion, and gave thee a just bias; in whatever form He wills, does He put thee together."

Islam and Christianity

"God has no son." "Jesus Christ is not God." "God has no partners." These statements appear to be direct contradiction of Christian teaching. At the same time they can be acceptable, depending on the interpretation, by a Christian. The statement "God has no son" was meant as a denial of God having taken a wife. There were many examples of Greek and

138

TABLE 4

Islam and Christianity

1. There is no free will (original sin)
2. Mary gave birth, with labour pains
3. A slave for a slave
4. Stoning to death for adultery
5. Cut off a limb for stealing
6. God does not speak to man
7. Permission for divorce
8. Religion includes politics
9. You may have four wives
10. Do not say Trinity
11. Jesus is not God
12. God has no Son
13. They did not crucify Christ

Islamic teaching contrasts with Christianity. The apparent differences between Islamic teaching and Christianity, depending in most cases on interpretation.

other gods being considered to have fathered sons in a human fashion. Also pagan beliefs involved gods coming down to earth to beget children. It is against this background that the denial in the Koran should be interpreted. Christianity teaches the spirit of Christ is the "son" of God. But no one claims that God was the human husband of Mary. Christians consider that Christ is spiritually the son of God in his perfection, that his spirit is the flowing out or emanation of the spirit of God and is thus part of the spirit of God. There is much misunderstanding in this field and this is evidenced by the many councils of the Christian church which discussed the Trinity and the relation between Christ and God. This relation may be considered to be at the very centre of comparative religions and also life science and religion.

The Koran was "revealed" following controversies within the Christian churches concerning the Trinity. The question at the center of this controversay was the "divinity" of Christ. It has been suggested that Christians worshipped Christ as they worshipped God and that they believed that Christ was God, the Creator. Some Moslems have suggested that Christians believe in two Gods and others that they believe in three. In truth, Christians worship God directly and through Christ and Mary. The word Trinity is taken to mean different things by different people. Translation, as elsewhere, introduces problems. In English Trinity is said to mean that there are three persons in God, whereas this is an improper translation. In the Koran the word used for Trinity means three thirds or divisions. This is not the Christian Trinity. In the Latin the word *persona* is the key to the meaning. *Persona* means personification or character. Life science can now explain the Christian trinity in simple terms. The Trinity implies that: 1) There is God who is one (united), 2) there is the universal spirit of God which becomes visible in space and time, and 3) there is the spirit of Christ which is divine in nature.

Christ did not claim to be God the Creator. He claimed unity with the Father. "The Father and I are one." This and other quotations in the Gospels clearly indicate his claim to divinity. Mark: 15.61: "Are you the Christ, the son of the Blessed. And Jesus said 'I am.' " Just as clearly he appeared to deny being God the Creator. When he said, "The Father is greater than I," he presumably meant that the father was not attached to the human body and that God the Father created the universe and mankind, whereas the essence of Christ's spirit is ("part" of) the essence of God.

The divinity of Christ is based on belief in his Incarnation by (the holy spirit of) God, his perfection, his forgiveness of sins, his miracles, his suffering unto death and his resurrection. Some people consider that the Incarnation is merely a tradition of early Christians and others cannot accept it because it makes God a "Father." From the scientific viewpoint the question is a problem of biology. A scientist considers the process of human development and asks the question, "Is divine Incarnation of Christ compatible with science?" The answer is not difficult. The change required is conversion of an X to a Y chromosome in a human female germ cell. Such a conversion can be compared in complexity to many chromosomal and genetic changes that are considered to have involved God's intervention in creative evolution. Thus some scientists propose that man developed from prehuman primates by loss of a pair of chromosomes, the number of these being reduced from 48 to 46. There are many genetic and chromosomal changes which could be described. Divine Incarnation is compatible with human biology. In a virgin birth fertilization requires that meiosis does not occur in an ovum and that radiation effects a chromosomal change from X to Y. The range of complexity involved is comparatively less than evolution of man from prehuman primates. Furthermore, there are at least seven substantial instances of virgin birth and modern research on cloning of cells supports the biological possibility of virgin birth. The description of the Incarnation is substantially the same or at least very similar in the Gospels and Koran. However, in the Koran Incarnation narrative, the Holy Spirit of God (of God and from God) is considered "sent" and not God. In Christianity the Holy Spirit is God appearing in time and space as a visible manifestation of God and is God.

The following is a model of the Christian trinity (see section on Christianity):

1) God as the source of radiation, including light (in the material world a parallel is the sun);

2) Christ represented by rays of light from the sun, formed of the same radiation and being an emanation or a flowing out of light;

3) The 'Holy' Spirit is the universal light or radiation directly from the source, from its rays and also through reflections and refraction. This universal spirit is everywhere. Thus radiation forms the same essence, of God, of Christ and the universal spirit.

This model serves to show that it is not claimed that Christ is God the Creator. Thus, the statement "Jesus is not God" is acceptable to Christians within this meaning. But Christian belief that Christ is divine and "true God from true God" is easily understood, using the model described. It is understood that the radiation which effected the incarnation of Christ remained in him as the spirit of God and that this spirit caused him to be divine since it was always present in his body. There is nowhere a reasonable claim that any other person combined perfection, miracles, forgiveness of sins, complete self-giving and unselfishness, suffering to death, and resurrection. The question of divine incarnation should not be taken in isolation but in the whole context of perfection, selflessness and spirituality.

Religion and Materialism

Islam is concerned with religion and a way of life. It thus relates to life in this world and prescribes laws and modes of behavior. The Koran includes some aspects of science, especially astronomy, agriculture and biology. It is claimed by some that references to human life science are embryological in nature. These extracts are compatible with early science.

Thus, for example, human sperm was said to have been converted into a clot of blood (XXIII, 14). This belief originated from the origin of blood in the uterus during human menstruation. Elsewhere it is implied that human germ cells are from the spinal region. Straining this statement in embryological terms is claimed to make it compatible with biology. The power of God is said to be reflected in creation, in rainfall and in providing for man. Man is encouraged in the Koran to enjoy life and to become attached to material things. Such an attitude is not found in Buddhism, Hinduism, or Christianity, which are concerned with non-attachment to material things.

Is God Father?

In Islam it is considered that God should not be called Father. The denial fits in with a similar one of God's "Sonship." It is considered that God cannot be given human attributes and that human characters do not apply to God. However, it must be admitted that there are many "human" words used in Islam and other religions to describe God. Examples are merciful, powerful, loving and peaceful. The prohibition of the word Father for God is against a background of pagan stories concerning gods having human (marriage) partners. The reason is that God should not be considered as indulging in human intercourse. However, there is no such belief among Christians, and according to scripture, the conception of Christ was by supernatural power. The omission of the word Father for God in Islam is clearly a denial of pagan ideas concerning God's "fatherhood." It seems to be thought by Muslims that Christians believe in God as an earthly father. This is not so. It is stated in the Koran (and not the four gospels) that the spirit of God came to Mary in the shape of a man. The Christian teaching is that supernatural force, e.g. radiation of a special type, came directly from God and was a part of God. Christianity also teaches that the eternal spirit of God, which was God and had been coexistent with God, was the spirit of Christ.

Jesus the Savior

The word Jesus means God the savior in Aramaic (Yeshua in Christ's language). The name Messiah is used for Jesus eleven times in the Koran. This word means the Lord, the Christ or the anointed one. It is understood that it referred to someone who was more than a prophet and who had a special, unique mission in relation to God's relation to man.

Elsewhere in the Koran Jesus is said to be only a prophet and it seems that this change was associated with altered relations between Moslems and Christians in the time of Muhammed. Many people, especially Jews, expected that the Messiah would be king and leader in politics. In Christianity the Messiah is believed to have preached a spiritual message only and not a political one.

Christ's principles were a reversal of the Old Testament,

with the promotion of infinite love and forgiveness and the saving of man from suffering.

An account of the incarnation of Jesus, in the Koran, is similar to that in the gospels. The account is consistent with the Christian ones; however, the Koran denies that Jesus is the son of God — presumably in a physical sense. Christianity is also in agreement with this.

III. 45, 46. "Behold the angels said, 'O Mary, God giveth thee glad tidings of a word from Him; his name will be Christ Jesus, the Son of Mary, held in honor in this world and the Hereafter and of (the company) of those nearest to God; He shall speak to the people in Childhood and in maturity. And he shall be (of the company) of the "righteous." ' "

XIX. 15. "She said, 'O my Lord, how shall I have a son when no man hath touched me?' He said, 'Even so, God createth what He willeth; when He hath decreed a plan, He but saith to it 'Be' and it is. And God will teach him the book and wisdom. The law and the gospel."

The following brief account of the birth of Jesus differs from the Christian one, which states that Mary gave birth to Jesus in a cave in Bethlehem. Life science supports the scripture of Genesis which states Eve (woman) would have stress in labor because of development of human knowledge, free will, original sin and stress in childbirth. Mary being perfect and "obedient" to God would not have original sin or its consequences stress in labor. The latter is the Christian tradition. At Lourdes, in an apparition, Mary said she was the "Immaculate Conception," meaning conceived without sin.

XIX. 22-37. "So she conceived him, and she retired with him to a remote place, and the pains of childbirth drove her to the trunk of a palm-tree."

The following quotation from the Koran apparently denies the physical sonship of Jesus, in relation to God, his "father." It should be understood that in the Christian belief, Jesus' sonship is spiritual, not physical. Thus Christianity agrees, in this sense, with this apparent denial of Jesus' "sonship."

XIX. 33. "So peace is on me the day I was born, the day that I die, and the day that I shall be raised up to life (again)."

144

XIX. 34. "Such (was) Jesus the son of Mary; (it is) a statement of truth, about which they (vainly) dispute, it is not befitting to (the majesty of) God that He should beget a son. Glory be to Him when He determines a matter He only says to it 'Be' and it is."

III. 59. "The similitude of Jesus before God is as that of Adam; he created him from dust, then said to him 'Be' and he was."

In this passage it seems that Christianity is favored. The fundamentals of Christian beliefs are rejected, however, in various parts of the Koran. Life science gives support to the Christian doctrine of original sin, as researched by the author.

III. 55. "Behold. God said, 'O Jesus, I will take thee and raise thee to Myself and clear thee (of the falsehood) of those who blaspheme; I will take those who follow thee superior to those who reject faith, to the day of Resurrection; then shall ye all return unto me, and I will judge between you and of the matters wherein ye dispute.' "

The evolutionists do not accept instant creation of man. Modern scientists are mainly on the side of evolution, versus instant creation or development by "chance." In the Christian scripture, Genesis, creation of Adam from dust and Eve from Adam's rib requires allegorical interpretation. Here, it is hardly possible to stretch allegory sufficiently for compatibility with the Koran.

The following "denial" of the crucifixion may be interpreted as a blunt, straight contradiction or else as referring to the spirit of God in Christ, which, being immortal, was raised up to God. Again there is a physical context and a spiritual one. Physically Christ "died," spiritually he lived and was "raised up."

IV. 157-158. "That they said (in boast), 'We killed Christ Jesus the son of Mary, The Apostle of God, — but they killed him not, nor crucified him, but so it was made to appear to them, and those who differ therein are full of doubts with no (certain) knowledge, but only conjecture to follow, for of a surety they killed him not: nay, God raised him up into himself; and God is exalted in power, wise."

According to Christianity, the spirit of God was God, in time and place. In this sense Jesus' Spirit was God, in time and place in Christ. The word Trinity in the Koran means three thirds and like "three persons" in Christianity does not convey the real meaning of the Trinity, which is three "aspects" or "characters" or "personalities" (Latin: personae) of God.

V. 49. "And in their footsteps we sent Jesus the son of Mary, confirming the law that had come before him: we sent him the gospel, therein was guidance and light, and confirmation of the law that had come before him; a guidance and an admonition to those who fear God."

IV. 171. "O People of the Book, commit no excesses in your religion: nor say of God aught but the truth, Christ Jesus the son of Mary was (no more than) an apostle of God, and his word. Which he bestowed on Mary, and a spirit proceeding from Him; so believe in God and His apostles. Say not 'Trinity,' desist: It will be better for you: for God is One God."

Some of the previous law, including the Commandments, was confirmed by Christ. Forgiveness was substituted for punishment, in teaching about adultery, theft, etc. Concerning a proposal that a woman accused of adultery be stoned, Christ said, "Let him among you who is without sin cast the first stone." And elsewhere the Christian God is personal and knowable; the Islam God remote.

"Love your enemies, do good to them that hate you." This is a reversal of the Old Testament doctrine and opposite to that in the Koran ("A slave for a slave"). God did not send Jesus the Gospel. The Gospels are an historical account of Jesus' life and actions, written by his contemporary Mark and others.

IX. 30. "The Jews call Uzair a son of God, and the Christians call Christ the son of God. That is a saying from their mouth; (in this) they but imitate what the unbelievers of old used to say God's curse be on them."

A change in the meaning of "Son of God" is implicit in the Christian concept of this designation. It means that Jesus' spirit is the spirit of God. Thus the Christians were accused in the Koran of "imitating" the pagans since they used the word

146

"son." The meaning, however, is different — spiritual, not physical.

The miracles of Jesus are fundamental in Christianity and were achieved (according to Christian belief) by the Spirit of God (from God — which is God) in Jesus. This is the very foundation of the divine nature of Christ and thus of the Trinity. There is an apparent contradiction of this in the following extract from the Koran:

V. 133. "Then will God say: 'O Jesus the son of Mary, recount my favor to thee and to thy mother. Behold. I strengthened thee with the holy spirit, so that thou didst speak to the people in childhood and in maturity. Behold. I taught thee the book and wisdom and the law and the gospel, and behold thou makest out of clay, as it were, the figure of a bird, by my leave, and thou healest those born blind, and the lepers, by my leave. And behold thou bringest forth the dead by my leave.' "

V. 119. "And behold God will say: 'O Jesus the son of Mary, didst thou say unto men, "Worship me and my mother as gods in derogation of God?" ' He will say, 'Glory to thee never could I say what I had no right (to say). Had I said such a thing, Thou wouldst indeed have known it.' "

Jesus and Mary are not worshipped as Gods, though this seems implied here. They are believed to be perfect and to have divine nature. The idea of separate gods was a pagan one. The implication in the Koran appears to be that Christians worship God the Creator or "Father," Jesus as God, and Mary as God (or Goddess). The three form a trinity and the denial of the Trinity appears to refer to this, which is not the Christian Trinity. The latter is:

a) God the Creator or Father,
b) God the Universal "Holy Spirit,"
c) The Spirit of God in Christ.

XIX. 23. "And the pains of childbirth drove her to the trunk of a palm tree; she cried (in her anguish) 'Ah would that I had died before this; would that I had been a thing forgotten and out of sight.' "

147

Our research in life science has shown a direct relation between stress hormone levels in late pregnancy and the duration of labor (congenital stress). Guilt or disobedience causes stress and in the Christian scripture Genesis, Eve was told she would suffer congenital stress in childbirth. According to Christian tradition based on St. Luke's Gospel Mary did not have congenital stress in giving birth to Jesus. Present teaching about Mary is that she was perfect and did not share "original sin." In the apparitions at Lourdes (in France) she said she is the Immaculate Conception. In the circumstances she would not suffer congenital stress, being free from the (original) "sin" or turning away from God that caused difficulty in birth. In Islam, however, original sin (based on free will and disobedience) is not accepted, though the sinlessness of Mary is.

XX. 91. "And (remember) her who guarded her chastity; we breathed into her of our spirit, and we made her and her son a sign for all people."

III. 42. "Behold the angels said: 'O Mary, God hath chosen thee and purified thee — chosen thee above the women of all nations.' "

The Crucifixion of Christ

It is stated in the Koran that Christ did not die on the Cross, but "it seemed that his likeness was crucified" or "it seemed like he was crucified." Different translations are available. The context of the crucifixion in the Koran is against a background opposite to that of Christianity. There is non-acceptance of the Christian teaching of original sin; thus no need for Christ's death and redemption of man. Taking the translation "his likeness was crucified," it is claimed that this originated in St. Barnabas' Gospel. This gospel is obviously very late since it is clearly written against the background of controversy concerning the Trinity. It contains a section where Christ is supposed to have reappeared to the virgin Mary and others and to have told them that he didn't really die on the cross but that Judas Iscariot had taken his place there. This late "gospel" is not accepted in Christianity and is considered heretical. In the same

148

section of the Koran concerning the crucifixion of Christ, it is stated that it seemed that the Jews killed him but that this was not actually so since God has predestined all things including his death. It seems that one should have an open mind on this section of the Koran in relation to Christianity. The Gospel of St. Barnabas does contain an outline description of the fall of man and original sin and it seems a contradiction that the crucifixion and redemption would be denied in the same scripture. The lateness of Barnabas' gospel and the obvious background of Christian heresies serve to explain this gospel. They also account for its non-acceptance by the Christian churches. It is difficult to date St. Barnabas' gospel but it seems to have been written hundreds of years later than the four accepted gospels (Mark, Matthew, Luke and John). These latter were written between 40 A.D. and 90 A.D., in the same generation as Christ. An alternative translation, "that it seemed like he died," is taken to mean, as explained in the text, that Christ was put up on the Cross and then taken up immediately to heaven, whereas he did not die. The background of this can be found elsewhere in the Koran, where it is stated that prophets do not die spiritually, but are assumed into heaven at the time of their (apparent) death. From the Christian viewpoint it is acceptable that Christ did not die spiritually. Therefore this section can be interpreted as supporting or denying Christ's crucifixion. It does not necessarily conflict with Christianity.

The Last Prophet

It is indicated in the Koran that Muhammed is the seal of the prophets. The meaning taken from this is that Muhammed was the last one to which the word of God was revealed. Another interpretation is a "confirmation" (rather than a final messenger) that Muhammed was to be the final arbiter concerning religious disputes among his followers. A prophet is taken to mean one who proclaims a divine message. If there is such a person as a final prophet this means that there is no need for further divine guidance of mankind. Therefore either

149

man has reached perfection or acquired all the knowledge necessary to become perfect. Clearly neither is true.

In science, knowledge is increasing all the time and there is constant expansion, especially in every branch of life science. It is apparent in life science that problems, including contraception, required divine guidance. One is forced to conclude that the reference to the last of the prophets refers to Islam alone. Christianity is not in the same line of religions nor is Judaism. One of Abraham's sons, Ismail, was the ancestor of the Arab people and another son, Isaac, of the Jews and Christians. It is acknowledged in the Koran that other religions contain truth and other scriptures had a divine origin. Both Hinduism and Christianity refer to the appearance of the Holy Spirit of God at various times when man needs guidance. It is claimed in the Bhagavadgita and the Christian gospels that the spirit of God appears at intervals to guide mankind and will do so until the end of time. It is also implicit in the Koran, in this reference to finality, that other interpretations are possible. These include Muhammed being a final arbiter in religion and other disputes among the Arab people.

Translation and Misunderstanding

The Koran, particularly among scriptures, is stated to be untranslatable precisely. This applies to every language and to all scriptures. At the same time, it is clear that there are no special problems about Arabic that do not apply to other languages as well. Meanings of words vary according to the individual concept as well as nationality, environment and education. For example, houses vary according to development of peoples, their way of life, climate, materials available, tradition and so on. Any word is understood in the context of a sentence, a paragraph, a book, literature, the subject it deals with, the state of human knowledge, individual intelligence and understanding. Thus when one person says a word another may understand a different meaning by it. There are special features of the life of a people who speak any particular language. The Arab people have relied particularly on language for their culture and until recently there has been little Westernization (with variety of culture and entertainment). The way of life of nomads and tribes in desert countries was limited and lacking in amenities; thus the language assumed a greater importance than in Western society. A literal translation is sometimes unsatisfactory and it is desirable that meaning be conveyed rather than word for word translations. This is difficult in the case of problems such as the Trinity, where a word cannot convey centuries of background discussion and conferences. A statement should not be related critically to another religion or judge its teaching, without explaining what it denies. Islam appears to deny many aspects of Christianity and for this reason it has been suggested that it is a mixture of Christian heresies. It is preferable that people learn the truth about other religions rather than criticize one another's beliefs, without any explanation or meaning.

What Is New in Islam?

V. 48. "We ordained therein for them: 'Life for life, eye for eye, nose for nose, ear for ear, tooth for tooth, and wounds equal for equal. But if any one remits the retaliation by way of charity, it is an act of charity, it is an act of atonement for himself. And if any fail to judge by (the light of) what God hath revealed they are (no better than) wrong doers.' "

V. 49. "And in the footsteps we sent Jesus the son of Mary, confirming the law that had come before him: we sent him the Gospel: therein was guidance and light and confirmation of the law that had come before him; a guidance and an admonition to those who fear God."

There is nothing new in the principles of Islam. The main development represented by Islam is a return to the strict monotheism of the Old Testament and a rejection of the fundamentals of Christianity. Otherwise it confirmed the old "eye for an eye" code for behavior, "slave for a slave and a woman

151

for a woman," severe punishment for theft, or adultery, and ease of divorce. Particularly rejected are the doctrines developed by Paul and John. Those were based on the teachings of human imperfection, redemption and divine nature (perfection) of Christ. Reference should be made here to the appearance of John the evangelist with Mary at Knock, Ireland in a vision seen by fifteen people. Mary's appearance with John indicated that she was giving her support to his gospel. The main contribution of John's gospel concerns the perfection or "divine nature" of Christ.

The reader is referred to the final chapter in this book, on Science and Apparitions. Mary asked an Egyptian to build a church. Later, when blessing this church as she promised, she prostrated herself in front of the Cross. Later appearances in Cairo were apparently intended to influence observers to favor Christ. It is a travesty of justice to state that Jesus "confirmed" the law that had come before him. In fact he rejected its principles and favored infinite love, forgiveness, healing and prevention of physical and psychological suffering. God did not send Jesus the gospel. The gospels were composed by the evangelists.

In life science the main aim is perfection, as in spirituality. This involves prevention of physical and psychological suffering. Healing is important in life science and in religion. There is little in the Koran related to suffering or to its prevention. What there is relates to Old Testament infliction of punishment. There is, however, an extract on suffering, as follows:

VII. 94-97. "Whenever we sent a prophet to a town, we took up its people in suffering and adversity, in order that they might learn humility. Then we changed their suffering into prosperity, until they grew and multiplied and began to say, 'Our fathers (too) were touched by suffering and affluence'... behold we called them to account of a sudden, while they realized not (their peril). If the people of the towns had but believed and feared God; we should indeed have opened out to them (all kinds of) blessings from heaven and earth; but they rejected (the truth). And we brought them to book for their misdeeds."

X. 99. "If it had been thy Lord's will, they would all have believed — all who are on earth. Wilt thou then compel mankind, against their will, to believe?"

The theme of predestination is a primitive one. Early man observed the alternation of night and day, the seasons, the repetitive nature of the phenomena of the universe and concluded these followed the plan of God. Similarly he concluded that man instinctually followed the will of God. This is in direct contradiction of "original sin" and its foundation, which is free will.

The following scripture appears to favor free will, and implies that man can choose good or evil, with severe punishment in "life after death."

XVIII. 29. "Say, 'The truth is from your Lord.' Let him who will, believe, and let him who will, reject (it): for the wrong-doers we have prepared a fire whose smoke and flames, like the walls and roof of a tent, will hem them in; if they implore relief they will be granted water like melted brass, that will scald their faces. How dreadful the drink, how uncomfortable a couch to recline on."

A further extract which is in favor of predestination is as follows:

LXXVI. 29, 30. "This is an admonition: Whosoever will, let him take a (straight) path to his Lord. But ye will not, except as God wills."

The quote "ye will not will, except as God wills" is in favor of predestination. The name Islam implies following the will of God and presumably includes predestination as a foundation for man's behavior. God's plan preceeded man — if man follows God's plan in all things, he is obedient to God (a Moslem). He is thus obeying God as he was predestined to do, in God's plan. According to Christianity man's intelligence and knowledge led to his free will and his "disobedience" in acquiring independence in decision of God's plan.

The Koran appears to be addressed to the Arab people in

153

some extracts. In the following it appears to be addressed to a wider audience.

LXXXI. 27-29. "Verily this is no less than a message to (all) the worlds. (With profit) to whoever among you wills to go straight; but ye shall not will except as God wills."

Laws in the Koran

Laws are prescribed about inheritance, crime and punishment. The Koran is not merely a book on religion but describes directions for social behavior. Moslems consider that these directions are for all humanity. Directions for marriage, divorce, retaliation, punishment, inheritance and so on are included in the Koran. A man may have up to four wives. Crime is punished by so many lashes of the whip, and adultery by stoning to death. Divorce is relatively easier than in other religions, it being only necessary to repeat, "I divorce thee" three times, to be divorced.

The inclusion in the Koran of laws and its dealing with material things means that it relates to this life as well as the next. Thus it offers a fairly complete guide as to behavior, and leaves little freedom to the individual. The combination of politics with religion contrasts with Christianity, which deals almost entirely with spirituality. A similar contrast applies to Hinduism. In this also the main idea is that man should strive for spiritual perfection and union with God. The attitude in the Koran is that man is or should be completely obedient to the directions of the Koran. When a Moslem follows directions of the Koran, he is then obedient. If he has never wavered from these directions he may be considered perfect. This contrasts with the imperfection of man, which is the theme of Christianity, whereas the ideal is to become perfect. A basic question, therefore, is whether man is perfect or imperfect.

Since the Koran deals with material things as well as with religion it is reasonable to expect that it can stand up to examination on material things, including science. Since it deals particularly with human behavior, then life science should have a preeminent position and provide principles that are universally applicable to all mankind. It is becoming clear that laws for a particular people may not suit others. A difficulty voiced by many is that the allowance of up to four wives is not in line with modern human population trends. Nor is theoretical ease of divorce conducive to stable marriage or proper upbringing of children. Stoning to death and cutting off limbs are not acceptable to civilized society. It is prescribed in the Koran that in retaliation by a family or individual for murder, a person of equal status may be killed in return. Thus a slave may be killed in retaliation for murder of a slave, a woman for a woman and so on. This whole concept is the same as that in the Old Testament (an eye for an eye) and is opposite to the principle of the Christian gospels.

The Koran: Changed or Unchanged?

Many suras were deleted from the Koran and replaced by new ones. This is implied in the text, in which God is considered to have stated that he was justified in deleting some verses and replacing them with new ones, considering he is capable of all things. One hears so much about the Koran being unchanged that this is an amazing feature. In the early days of Islam many copies and versions remained. Critics of both Islam and Christianity refer to the denunciation and prohibition of some copies of the Koran or Gospels. Many Moslems believe that the teaching of Christianity has changed due to councils of the Church, etc. Christians consider that changes in the Koran are not compatible with the claim of this book originating as a revelation from God. Many Moslems defend changes in the Koran by saying that God made various statements at different times and in different circumstances. As the latter changed the advice and prescribed laws are considered to be changed also. In other words, God changed His mind. This is difficult to accept in view of God being all-knowing.

The concepts of heaven and hell are probably nowhere so explicitly portrayed as in the Koran, including the following extracts:

III. 15. "Say: Shall I give you glad tidings of things far better than those? For the righteous are Gardens in nearness to their Lord, with rivers flowing beneath; therein is their eternal home; with companions pure (and holy): and the good pleasure of God, for in God's sight are (all) his servants.' "

IV. 56. "Those who reject our signs, we shall soon cast into the fire, as often as their skins are roasted through. We shall change them for fresh skins, that they may taste the penalty: for God is exalted in power, wise."

XIV. 16, 17. "In front of such a one is Hell, and he is given for drink boiling fetid water. In gulps will he sip it, but never will he be near swallowing it down his throat."

Face of God

The "face of God" is referred to in the following extracts, indicating the personal nature of God in Islam, as in other religions. The ninety-nine characters of God are also "personal." The "face of God" is mentioned in a number of suras.

VI. 52 "Send not away those who call on their Lord morning and evening, seeking His face."

XVIII. 28. "And keep thy soul content with those who call in their Lord morning and evening, seeking His face."

LV. 26-27. "All that is on earth will perish; but will abide (for ever) the face of thy Lord, full of majesty, bounty and honor."

God

The incomprehensible and omnipotent nature of God is stressed in the Koran. There is emphasis also on "life after living."

V. 103. "No vision can grasp Him, but His grasp is over all vision: He is above all comprehension, yet is acquainted with all things."

VI. 31. "Lost indeed are they who treat it as a falsehood that they must meet God — until on a sudden the hour is on them, and they say, 'Ah woe is unto us that we took no thought of it.' "

There is "one" God according to Islam, and thus not "spirit of God" (being God) in Jesus Christ.

CXII. 1-4. "Say: He is God the one and only: God, the eternal absolute; He begetteth not, nor is He begotten, and there is none like unto him."

II. 255. "God, there is no God, but He, the living, The self-subsiding eternal."

XXIII. 92. "He knows what is hidden and what is open: too high is he for the partners they attribute to Him."

The "One God" of Islam cannot have partners.

IV. 85. "Yet whoever recommends and helps a good cause becomes a partner therein; and whoever recommends and helps an evil cause, shares in its burden."

The general denial of the physical fatherhood of God is specifically applied to Christianity. Only elementary knowledge of Christianity is required to understand that Jesus is the "Son of God" in a spiritual sense.

II. 116. "They say, 'God hath begotten a son, Glory be to Him.' Nay, to Him belongs all that is in the heavens and on earth: everything renders worship to Him."

V. 75. "They do blaspheme who say: 'God is Christ the son of Mary.' But said Christ, 'O Children of Israel, worship God, my Lord and your Lord.' Whoever joins other Gods with God, God will forbid him the Garden, and the Fire will be his abode. There will, for the wrong- doers, be no one to help."

VI. 101. "To him is due the primal origin of the Heavens and the earth. How can He have a son when He hath no consort? He created all things."

XXIII. 91, 92. "No son did God beget nor is there any god along with him; (if there were many gods), behold, each god would have taken away what he had created, and some would have Lorded it over others."

The principle is division among two masters (you cannot

157

serve God and Mammon, the world) is similar to that expounded here. It was used by Jesus as an argument to separate spirituality of religion from materialism.

VI. 19. "Say, 'What thing is most weighty in evidence?' Say, 'God is witness between me and you; this Koran hath been revealed to me by inspiration, that I may warn you and all whom it reaches. Can ye possibly bear witness that besides God there is another God?' Say: 'Nay. I cannot bear witness.' Say, 'But in truth He is the One God. And I truly am innocent of (your blasphemy of) joining others from Him.' "

From the point of view of life science, the following extract represents a very old human idea of God.

XXV. 61, 62. "Blessed is He who made constellations in the skies, and placed therein a lamp and a moon giving light; and it is He who made the night and the day to follow each other."

There is no other God but "Allah." God has no partners. God is not divided. God is united and everywhere. He is also merciful and forgiving, but he will punish evildoers with eternal fire. Science uses numbers for counting and for limiting as well as for dividing materials. One is a number and limits, in its human meaning, anything which it describes. Science could not agree with the unqualified statement "there is one God." It is quite different to say, "God is one." This means that God is united in all his "parts or areas or qualities or essence." But the statement "God is one" is compatible with the scientific opinion of God, that God is infinite or absolute. It is frequently stated by Moslems that one should not apply human terms to God, since these are human in meaning and in application and they ascribe human qualities to God.

Marriage and Divorce

IV. 3. "If ye fear that ye shall not be able to deal justly with the orphans, marry women of your choice. Two, three, or four, but if ye fear that ye shall not be able to deal justly (with them), then only one or (if captive) that your right hands possess."

V. 6. "This day are (all) things good and pure made lawful

unto you. The food of the people of the book is lawful unto you and yours is lawful unto them. (Lawful unto you in marriage) are (not only) chaste women who are believers, but chaste women among the people of the book."

A Moslem man may marry a Christian woman, but a Moslem woman may not marry a Christian man. Fatima was one of the exceptions (see last chapter).

XXIV. 2, 3. "The woman and the man guilty of adultery or fornication — flog each of them with a hundred stripes. Let not compassion move you."

II. 228. "Divorced women shall wait concerning themselves for three monthly periods, nor is it lawful for them to hide what hath created in their wombs, if they have faith in God and the last day and their husbands have the better right to take them back in that period, if they wish for reconciliation. And women shall have rights similar to the rights against them, according to what is equitable; but men have a degree (of advantage) over them. And God is exalted in power, wise."

"I divorce thee" repeated three times constitutes the requirement for divorce in Islam. In various Islamic countries there is legislation which makes it more difficult than this requirement. The divorced wife must be compensated materially for loss of marital status, with associated "protection" and rights.

Contraception

The "natural law" is the basis for the teaching, general in Islam, that artificial contraception is immoral. The prophet Muhammed is said, in tradition (Hadith), to have allowed coitus interruptus or incomplete intercourse. Research has shown that the latter, as well as artificial contraceptives, is apparently responsible for 50% of all cases of breast cancer. This is explained by a protective function of male hormones in seminal secretions. On the basis of this and of principles of "natural law" life science does not support coitus interruptus or artificial contraception. Life science is, in principle, opposed to hormonal contraceptives ("the pill") on the basis of

159

their harmful effects on health. These effects involve human maldevelopment, changes in immunity, stress and cancer.

Mary Was Without Sin

The meaning of the Immaculate Conception is that the virgin Mary (Miriam) was born without sin. This is supported by the Koran insofar as it states that she was without sin. In Christianity the doctrine of the Immaculate Conception took centuries to develop and the basis of this belief was the need for her to be conceived without sin if her Son was to have a divine nature. The description of the Nativity by Luke and also the early tradition of the Fathers of the Church held that Mary gave birth to Jesus without stress. This can now be understood and her unique human obedience is compatible with the Christian churches' teaching that she was without sin. The statement in the Koran shows general agreement with Christian teaching on this point; but no reason is given, such as is found in Christianity (complete obedience to God's will).

Reproductive Behavior

II. 222. "They ask thee concerning women's courses. Say, They are hurt and a pollution: so keep away from women in their courses; and do not approach them until they are clean. But when they have purified themselves, ye may approach them in any manner, time, or place ordained for you by God."

There is scriptural "permission" for intercourse except at menstruation. There is no acknowledgement of the difference in reproductive pattern, in the human species, on a comparative basis. In Christianity there is recognition of (development of) a sexual pattern in human development which is unique in man. This pattern follows the concept of "free will," which man developed (in association with intelligence). It is considered to be a part of "original sin." In life science it is a recognized part of early human development, and contrasts with other species where mating is normally practiced only at oestrus.

160

Free Will and Original Sin

The difference between Islam and Christianity on original sin, based on free will, is fundamental. This is because Christianity implies human imperfection and the need for redemption. This concept can be found in Genesis, in the Old Testament, in the Gospels and in Paul's epistles. If man is imperfect then he is incapable of his own accord of becoming perfect. Only by God's grace can man possibly attain such a state. In Islam, obedience implies human perfection. It is based on action in direct relation to God's command, and it implies that man is perfect; therefore there is no need for redemption (e.g. by Christ). Other basic features of Christianity which are directly related to human free will and (freedom from) original sin are the Immaculate Conception of Mary (who gave birth to Jesus, without congenital stress, according to early Christian tradition), the divine character of Christ and his physical death on the cross.

Original sin is based on scripture and is simple disobedience due to intelligence, knowledge and resulting free will. Because of this Eve was promised that she would bring forth her children in congenital stress, which is difficulty in labor. It has now become possible to investigate the cause of human congenital stress. It has been found in our laboratory that there is a direct relation between blood levels of human stress hormones (ACTH) and cortisol in late pregnancy and the duration of human labor. No such relation was found for output of the reproductive oestriol hormone. This finding supports psychosomatic determination of human congenital distress and thus original sin.

There is a description of the "Fall" of Adam and Eve in the Koran. The story of partaking of a tree of knowledge or its fruit is similar to the two religions. There are minor differences but it is implied in both that Adam and Eve became imperfect (the fall), whereas they were created perfect.

In Genesis and Christianity the imperfection of man is a human characteristic, following upon the "disobedience" of Adam and Eve. Their free will and potential for evil led to the

161

doctrine of original sin, which means that man's independence of God in his free will is necessarily evil. In Islam original sin is not accepted. Thus children are considered to be born without sin but to develop the tendency or the possibility for evil at some later stage.

The problem here is free will versus predestination. If man has free will and if this is the most important factor in human potential for evil, then life science may be said to be on the side of "original sin." If all things are predestined, as is broadly indicated in the Koran, then original sin would not be acceptable since it would be ascribed directly to God. It is clear that one cannot ascribe evil to God, or to planning or predestination, since this would completely contradict sin as such. This is in contrast with Christianity, which accepts free will, human imperfection and absence of human obedience to God's will. Thus evil is caused by human intelligence and free will.

Islamic teaching excludes "original sin," which is the basis of Christianity. It means development of intelligence by man, and therefore the potential for evil, which is considered evil in itself. Sin means a "turning away" from God, and man's free will (and therefore independence of God, in decisions) means that he is not necessarily following God's will.

According to the literal meaning, Christians are imperfect since they are human (finite in all things, imperfect), whereas Moslems are not considered imperfect (presuming they live up to the name of their religion and do God's will). The main feature of the present investigation is evidence supporting the account of original sin given in Genesis. An incidental observation relates to apparitions of Mary, who clearly sides with Christian beliefs and attitudes (see chapter on apparitions). Her request in Egypt was for the building of a church (see final chapter).

In life science the outstanding development has been the mind of man. Similarly, there have developed, in association with this, philosophy, religion, logic, psychology and physiology of the brain. Religion is based in the mind of man, on his emotions and reason.

Whereas reason is used in the Koran to prove God's ex-

162

istence as a creator, human mental development (the tree of knowledge) is not the foundation stone of Islam, as it is of Christianity. Christianity blames man's mental freedom for his tendency to evil and calls this tendency Original Sin. Islam does not use the same basis, though acknowledging the existence of good and evil.

Islam is based primarily on the Koran, whereas Christianity is based on human mental development, as described in Genesis. However, the Garden of Eden is referred to in the Koran (II, 30-39) and Adam and Eve, tempted by the devil, fell from their state of happiness and came to know evil. Thus the scripture is similar to the Christian one in Genesis, in which the foundation is the concept of man's independence and original sin. In Islam the episode of Adam and Eve is rejected as the main basis for religion, and also all the Christian fundamentals based on the "fall" of Adam and Eve — except the Immaculate Conception of Mary.

Miriam in Cairo

Reference to the many appearances of Miriam (Mary) in Cairo is appropriate here, since many people believe she tried to influence Moslems in the direction of Christianity. In 1920 she appeared in a dream to a member of the Khalil Ibrahim family, who owned a vacant site at Zeitun, near Cairo. She asked him to build a church on the site and promised to bless it in about 50 years. She appeared on many occasions from 1968 to 1970 and millions of people witnessed the apparition, many taking photographs. A large number of people, including many Moslems, were cured of diseases and the cures were confirmed by panels of medical experts. The final chapter of this book is devoted to science and apparitions, including those at Zeitun.

CHAPTER 8

CHRISTIANITY, HEALING AND PERFECTION

The main features are that Christianity is based on human development of intelligence and knowledge, and that, due to this, man has free will, and makes decisions of his own and independently of God (disobedience; original sin); as a result of this man is born in congenital stress; Jesus (meaning God is savior) was the spiritual son of God in his perfection. A voice from heaven, at his baptism, was heard to say, "Thou art my beloved son, with thee I am well pleased." Jesus preached and healed the sick: he was crucified and arose from the dead appearing to the apostles and others. He said that his spirit, the spirit of God (Greek: *Paracletos*), would be a counsellor to man until the end of the world. In Islam *Paracletos* is considered to refer to Muhammed.

Christianity aims at avoiding suffering, at healing, and perfection. It was summarized by Jesus Christ as commanding men to "Love God, and love your neighbor as yourselves." The Christian trinity is the spirit of God in Jesus, the universal spirit of God, and the spirit of God the Creator (Father). This spirit is the same "essence of perfection" and is not divided — God is one, meaning there is unity of the spirit of God. Jesus did not claim there is one numerical God. Christianity teaches that man is imperfect, because of his free will, and that mankind should aim at perfection and spirituality.

An important theme of Christianity, i.e. "original sin," resulted in congenital stress, according to scripture. Medical research has now confirmed psychosomatic aspects of human development and of stress in childbirth as evidenced by blood levels of stress hormones. This evidence supports "original sin."

Christianity is about perfection, physical, mental and spiritual. In general, anything "made" or finite is not perfect; according to scripture the only perfect being is God. The only perfect human beings (according to Christianity) were the virgin Mary and Christ. Christianity is a pure religon, i.e. it does not include a political system. However, a summary of philosophy of living given by Christ was "Love God and Your Neighbor." Thus it commands love and respect for man as well as God. Christ spoke of "the Kingdom of Heaven." This is the perfection of mentality and consciousness. In Christianity it is believed that man is not perfect and that his state of imperfection is due to human intelligence, free will, a potential for evil, and therefore "disobedience" or the lack of instinctual obedience to God's will. This free will and "independence in decision" of God or "disobedience" is called "original sin" or turning away from God's will. In contrast, Moslem means being obedient to God, and thus perfect.

Christianity is the religion with a most comprehensive attitude and clear policy towards suffering; it aims at putting an end to suffering, and meantime, healing the wounds of physical, psychological and spiritual ills. It aims at its prevention by "salvation" in Christ's death; involves healing of mind, body and soul; exhorts bearing with suffering if this must be done; engenders "love of others" and compassion in their suffering; endows everyone with the potential of becoming spiritual "sons of God" and thus, in a sense, His partners, carrying out His will and being instruments of His creation. Reference to "sons of God" and "partners" does not imply

166

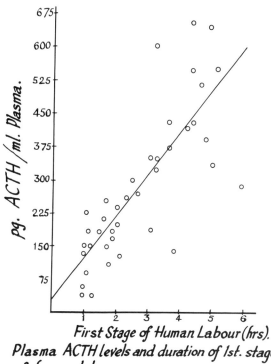

First Stage of Human Labour (hrs).
Plasma ACTH levels and duration of 1st. stage
of human labour .

Figure 6

Stress hormone ACTH in blood in late pregnancy, in relation to duration of subsequent labor. Levels of ACTH,
cortisol and VMA in late pregnancy have been found to
be linearly related to the subsequent duration of human
labor. In combination, these results support a
psychosomatic cause for human difficulty in childbirth.
These findings support the promise to Eve, in Genesis,
"Thou shalt bring forth children in suffering." Scientific
measures of parameters of stress support the text of
Genesis, and the concepts of the "Fall" and of "Original
Sin." VMA is formed from adrenaline, noradrenaline and
dopamine.

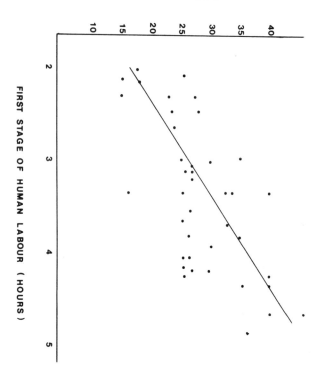

Figure 7

Stress hormone (cortisol) in blood, in late pregnancy, in relation to duration of subsequent human labor. The inter- pretation is similar to that for Fig. 6, supporting the "Fall" and "Original Sin.".

equality with God the Creator; the meaning is doing the will of God, which is the abolishment of suffering and of its causes, including sin, which is offense to God and to mankind, His creation.

Man is particularly prone to psychological stress since man's intelligence is more developed than that of other species. Because of man's knowledge and ingenuity he is especially capable of causing suffering to his fellowmen, or to other forms of life. The process of healing is of similar complexity to creative evolution. Duration of healing depends on the size of a wound or infected area, on age, diet, vitamins, hormones and other factors. Healing in injury or disease depends on biological reactions. It involves white blood cells which ingest and break down foreign material, and also general and specific antibodies (in relation to the particular infection or tumor). Gamma globulins and other plasma proteins are involved and they derive from lymphocytes and plasma cells. Control of healing is by various factors, including steroid hormones. The process of healing requires activity of cells, DNA and other substances, as well as phagocytosis. Among religions, Christiantiy is especially associated with healing in miracles by Christ and his mother. Recent miracles by Our Lord's mother at Zeitun have been confirmed by medical experts and are clearly supernatural. There have been many others in Lourdes, Guadelupe, Knock, Fatima, and in other places where Mary appeared.

The principles of Christianity are opposite to materialist: This may account for their unpopularity in politics, whose business it is to deal with material things. The principles of Christianity counter the human, selfish nature of man. It can be expected that they meet with unpopularity, being spiritual and against man's natural tendency, which is independence of God in free will (Original Sin) and in imperfection. Self- consciousness and selfishness are the basis of human imperfection; unselfishness is the distinctive principle of Christianity. The human quality of selfishness is implied in Genesis: Hindusim and Buddhism share the common foundation of aversion to materialism. Complete unselfishness was a character of Christ

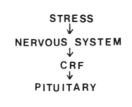

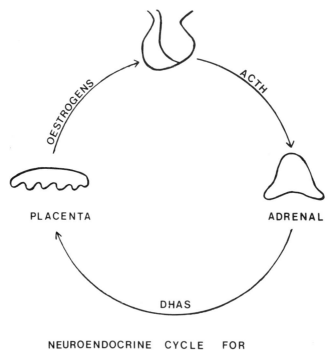

NEUROENDOCRINE CYCLE FOR
HUMAN OESTRIOL PRODUCTION

Figure 8

Neuroendocrine cycle proposed for human pregnancy
whereby oestrogens stimulate stress hormone production. This cycle is considered to contribute to the profound change in hormone pattern in human pregnancy,
and to congenital stress (difficulty in childbirth).

and, with healing and perfection, forms a triad of Christian objectives.

Christianity teaches that Jesus was the spiritual son of God as well as a man, that he was born of the virgin Mary, performed miraculous cures and forgave sins (by the power of God's spirit in him), was crucified and arose from the dead. The meaning of Jesus in Aramaic, Christ's native language, is savior. The spirit of God has "descended" from heaven when man needed guidance and courage on a number of special occasions since then, when man needed guidance in the right path. Christ promised that the "spirit of God" (Greek: *Parakletos:* English: Paraclete), meaning counsellor, shall be with mankind until the "end of the world"; Christianity does not teach that Christ is God the Creator, that God was Christ's Father and that Christ was God's Son begotten in a human manner.

The objective in medicine is healing and the aim of medical practice and research is to help "our neighbor" physically. There is often a psychological component as well as physical disease to be dealt with. Medicine and Christianity have similar objectives. They require a similar mentality. The Old Testament dictum of "an eye for an eye and a tooth for a tooth" was primitive, aggressive and almost prehuman and is superseded by benevolence and good will in the medical and Christian ideal. Christ countered primitive laws with principles which are the basis for civilization.

There is a similarity in meaning between "healing," "saving" and "redeeming." The aim of all three is to preserve or reclaim wholeness, health and perfection. They may apply physically, psychologically or spiritually. Forgiveness of sins restores perfection to the soul and is spiritual healing. Healing in Christianity involves all aspects of restoration of health, of body, of mind, and of soul. Christianity aims at perfection — and implies the existence of imperfection, part of which is "disobedience" of the human mind. The perfection of Christ and of his mother was an example for humanity and His "way" is through love and healing.

The imperfection of humanity has been selfishness originating in human self-consciousness. Healing, psychological and spiritual, involves love of God and of one's neighbor. Healing of the mind and soul requires an "opening" and turning outward of the mind toward God and man. This is the opposite of the introspective mind of selfishness, and requires "love of others" to be substituted for "self-love." Christianity involves, par excellence, healing of body, mind and soul. Saving and healing have similar meanings, both aiming at perfection and prevention of imperfection which is the basis of suffering.

Medical science and practice have similar aims to Christian physical healing and medical research has now shown the importance of stress hormones in childbirth, immunity and a variety of diseases, physical and psychiatric. The present investigation reports results of such research by the author and explains the central role of human intelligence and free will (the original sin of Christianity; turning away from God, independence) in determining susceptibility to stress and suffering. Stress and suffering form central themes of Buddhism and Christianity. In Buddhism, being born and giving birth, aging, disease and dying all involve suffering, and the main solution is withdrawal of sensation by meditation. In Christianity Christ practiced physical and spiritual healing and he suffered passion and death on a cross. In Genesis Eve was told by God she would suffer distress in Childbirth, because of her "disobedience" to God. There is tradition that both Buddha and Christ were born without stress of labor; Buddha is sometimes depicted, however, as being born through his mother's side hip. There is tradition and scripture that Christ's mother was a virgin, without sin, i.e. obedient to the will of God. The attitude of Christianity is to "work" on suffering, to prevent causes of suffering and to heal the "scars" when it has occurred. Also, Christ's death is given a special meaning, in saving mankind from suffering.

According to Christianity man is imperfect and the aim of man should be perfection. The "love of neighbor" is extended to social work (as well as material things). Helping the socially and physically deprived and healing the sick are roles associated more with principle in life science and in spirituality

172

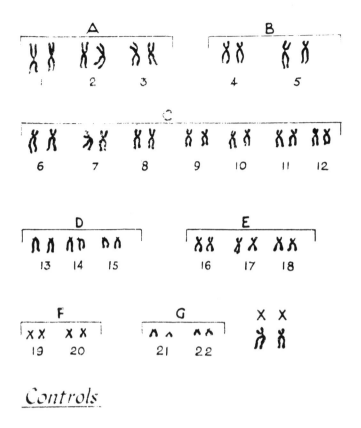

Figure 9

Human chromosomes. The normal complement is 46 XX in females and 46 XY in males. An ovum contains 23 X. Virginal fertilization, giving birth to a son, would require formation of a Y chromosome since these are located in male germ cells.

concerning perfection. Perfection of human physical form leads to a normal life span and imperfection leads to disease and to death. Imperfection in spiritual matters is believed to lead to a spiritual death and perfection to "eternal life."

The question of the perfection or divine character of Christ raises another — that he should be born of a mother who was perfect. The early tradition of Christianity included the teaching that Mary gave birth to Christ without difficulty or "congenital stress." The description in Luke's Gospel apparently supports this, "She gave birth to her first born son and wrapped him in swaddling clothes and laid him in a manger." Congenital stress was stated in Genesis to be the fate of Eve (woman) because of original sin. "You will bring forth children in congenital stress." (Sometimes translations give the word "pain" instead of stress.) Examination of the scripture in various parts of Genesis, etc. shows stress or distress to be the most suitable translation. Mary is believed, in Christianity, to have been without sin, and is called "The Immaculate Conception." In the Koran, however, Mary is stated to have had pains at the birth of Christ. "And the pains of childbirth drove her to the trunk of a palm tree" (XIX. 23).

This would appear to contradict her Immaculate Conception. Also, however, from the Koran the following extract supports her virginity and sinlessness. "And remember her who guarded her chastity; we breathed into her of our spirit, and we made her and her son a sign for all people" (XXI. 91).

A basic theme of Christianity, the "sonship of Christ," can be supported or denied, according to meaning. There is agreement that Christ was not a physical son of God (humanly conceived). There is also agreement that Christ was brought into being by a spirit of God, from God. "We breathed into her of our spirit" (Koran, XXI, 91). The question then is whether "our spirit" was divine, i.e. of God, from God. A part, as it were, of God is God. The spirit of God becoming the spirit of Christ was claimed to be divine and "part of God" though not all of God (i.e. God the origin of all things, the Creator or Father). She said, "O my Lord, how shall I have a son when no man hath touched Me?" He said, "Even so, God createth what

TABLE 5

Environmental Factors Affecting or Reflecting Mentality

1.	Living Conditions	Housing, architecture, materials, Furniture & Equipment, Water & Waste.
2.	Education	Primary, Secondary, Third level, Availability, Literacy.
3.	Agriculture	Crops & animals, Methods.
4.	Transport	Roads, Railways, Airports and Airlines.
5.	Medicine	Medical Schools & Hospitals, Nursing Schools, Doctors & Assistants. Diseases - Endemic. Health.
6.	Social Life	Amenities, Museums, Theatres & Cinemas, Art Galleries, Functions, Lectures (public), Meetings & Meeting Places.
7.	Recreation	Games, Clubs, Participation.
8.	Literature	General - Prose, Poetry. Current. Newspapers & Magazines. Libraries, Writers, Talks & Discussions.
9.	Drama, Music Dance	Theatres, Societies, Halls, Artists, Performances, Television & Radio,
10.	Nature	Scenery, Trees, Mountains, Waters, Grass, Lakes & Rivers, Shrubs, Flowers, Animals & Plants.
11.	Religions	World & Other Religions, Places of Worship, Practices & Laws.
12.	Politics	Political System & Control, Freedom — Regulations.
13.	Geography	Climate, Terrain, Natural Hazards.
14.	Economics	Incomes, Employment.
15.	Food	Nutrition, Physique.
16.	Games	Outdoor & Indoor, Athletics
17.	Industrial Development	Technology
18.	Customs	Festivals. Traditions. Dress.
19.	Historical Buildings	Antiques.
20.	Home Industries	Crafts & Materials.

Religion and mentality are affected by environment, and have a reciprocal interaction. Mentality is affected and determined by many factors, as indicated.

175

He willeth: when He hath decreed a plan, He but saith to it 'Be' and it is." This seems to imply that Christ was created, as in Aryanism. Christ is implied to be "made" and to exist from that time. Biologically, Christ was physically "made" by formation of a Y chromosome in a single germ cell. The implications of a definite instant creation ("Be and it is") is not accepted by Evolution except at a chromosomal level. Life science does not accept that a man can be created instantaneously. It is clear that one cannot accept the Koran and also Evolution. One must choose one or the other. Which one a person accepts depends on environment, intelligence and education. A primitive, uneducated society does not have a choice. The future education of the masses in science will largely determine what beliefs can be seen to be compatible with science. Knowledge, life science and truth shall see to it that false hypotheses or statements will not survive.

The Trinity, its meaning and understanding are simple and not a mystery to those who accept that in the incarnation of Christ the Y chromosome was formed by the spirit of God, in the absence of Y from a human father. The perfection of the Y chromosome in Christ is reflected in absence of aggression (now associated with Y). Also, in division of a maternal germ cell, an X chromosome was broken down. Thus, an X was replaced by a Y. Thus Christ was divine in being spiritually the "spirit of God, from God." The inclusion of Jesus in the Trinity is because he is unique, the "only" spiritual son in being perfect and above all others. The Holy Ghost is the universal spirit of Christianity.

A model will explain the Trinity for the layman. If the essence of God were light and God represented as the sun, then the rays of the sun represent Christ. The universal light, reflected from the sun and from its rays, represents the universal spirit.

Since the purpose of this book is explanation rather than factual teaching, it is proposed that only a few extracts be quoted from the original gospel. The gospel quoted here is that according to St. Mark. St. Mark was one of the seventy sent forth to preach by Christ after the resurrection, when

TABLE 6

Duration of labor in different species.

Species	Duration of Labor
Mare	5 - 15 min.
Rabbit	10 min.
Sheep	15 min.
Pig, cat, dog	10 - 30 min.
Rhesus and squirrel monkeys	1 hour
Cow	2 hours
Chimpanzee	4 hours
Human	14 hours

Eve, representing womankind, was promised difficulty in childbirth (Genesis 3, 16). The figures shown indicate relative durations of labor in different species, and thus an important measure of the stress of labor. Blood levels of stress hormones ACTH and cortisol (measured before labor) have been shown by the author to be directly related to the duration of human labor. This evidence is in favor of a psychosomatic cause, in human development, of human difficulty in childbirth, supporting Genesis and original sin. Traditional teaching is that Mary was free from original sin and did not have a difficult childbirth at the birth of Christ.

Christ appeared to the apostles in the upper room of Mark's mother's house.

Mark's gospel was written between 50 and 60 A.D. in Rome. Mark's was the first gospel and the others are partly based on it. It is believed to be accurate, Mark being a contemporary of Jesus and a friend of Peter: his mother was a close friend of Mary. It was based on teachings of Peter, who spent much time with Jesus. This gospel was written in Greek, for a non-Jewish, Greek-speaking population. Mark's family was Jewish, from Cyrene (Libya) and migrated to Palestine a short time before the birth of Jesus. The last supper and the appearance of the Holy Spirit to the twelve, on Pentecost, took place respectively in the houses of Mark and of his mother. St. Mark's mother was with Mary, Jesus' mother, at the crucifixion, death and burial of Christ. Mark went to Egypt about 43 A.D., soon after Christ's death and started a church in Alexandria. He went back to Jerusalem in 49 A.D. to attend the first Church Council, the Council of Jerusalem. After the council he returned to Egypt and Alexandria. He was martyred in 68 A.D. He established the Christian Coptic church known as the church of Alexandria.

"The beginning of the Gospel of Jesus Christ, the son of God. As it is written in Isaiah the prophet,...."

"Behold I send my messenger before thy face, who shall prepare the way — the voice of one crying in the wilderness; Prepare the way of the Lord. Make his paths straight." (Mark I: 1-3.)

"John the Baptizer appeared in the wilderness, preaching a baptism of repentance for the forgiveness of sins, and there went out to him all the country of Judea, and all the people of Jerusalem and they were baptized by him in the River Jordan, confessing their sins. Now John was clothed with camel's hair, and had a leather girdle around his waist, and ate locusts and wild honey, and he preached saying, 'After me comes he who is mightier than I, the thong of whose sandals I am not worthy to stoop down and untie. I have baptized you with water; but he will baptize you with the Holy Spirit.' " (I: 4-8.)

"In those days Jesus came from Nazareth of Galilee and was

178

baptized by John in the Jordan. And when he came up out of the water, immediately he saw the heavens opened and the Spirit descending upon him like a dove; and a voice came from heaven: 'Thou art my beloved Son with thee I am well pleased.' " (I: 11.)

The meaning of the Aramaic word for Jesus is Savior.

"Thou art my beloved son" appears to directly contradict the statement in the Koran. In fact it does not do so.

"The Jews call Uzair a son of God, and the Christians call Christ the Son of God. That is saying from their mouth; (in this) they but imitate what the Unbelievers of old used to say. God's curse be on them — how they are deluded away from the truth; they take their priests and their anchorites to be their lords in derogation of God, and (they take as their Lord) Christ the son of Mary; yet they were commanded to worship but one God; there is no god but He. Praise and glory to Him: (far is He) from having the partners they associate (with Him)." (Koran IX 30-31.)

The sonship of Christ is a problem for many, due to misunderstanding. In Christianity God is believed to have a son spiritually; he is not considered to have been a father in the human way through reproduction.

The implication in Mark's gospel that God spoke and was audible contrasts with the Moslem belief about the Koran that God does not speak, but communicated in an unknown fashion (Arabic) to the Angel Gabriel who, having a voice, spoke to Muhammed. Both Christians and Moslems believe that God spoke to Moses. The meaning of the word "Son," as of almost any word, may differ. Thus both the following two statements are true.

(1) God has no Son;

(2) God has a Son;

(1) in the human sense of father and son;

(2) in the special sense of Christ, the spirit of God replacing a Y chromosome. Formation of a Y chromosome is less complex biologically than X or other chromosomes since Y is simpler, more repetitive in chemistry, and carries little genetic information, apart from determination of male sexuality.

179

The word father and son means that a son is formed from part of his father — in human procreation, from a germ cell. In the same way God was not a father humanly, but spiritually, in that Jesus' spirit, being perfect from conception was "a part of" the universal spirit, truth and love, and in this way Jesus was a spiritual son of God.

"And they went into Caphernaum; and immediately on the sabbath they entered the synagogue and taught. And they were astonished at his teaching, for he taught them as one who had authority, and not as the scribes. And immediately there was in their synagogue a man with an unclean spirit — and he cried out, 'What, have you come to destroy us? I know who you are, the Holy One of God.' But Jesus rebuked him saying, 'Be silent, and come out of him.' And the unclean spirit, convulsing him and crying with a loud voice, came out of him. And they were all amazed, so that they questioned among themselves, saying, 'What is this? A new teaching with authority, he commands even the unclean spirits, and they obey him.' " (Mark I: 21-27.)

The authority of Christ is central to his divine nature, i.e. his "Sonship" of God. He cast out spirits, according to the Gospels, by his own command. Similarly his miracles were by his own authority, i.e. by the spirit of God in him. Thus his spirit was the spirit of God and he described himself as "Son of man," to indicate that he had human as well as divine nature. The phrase "Son of Man" was often used by Jesus to describe himself since this performance of miracles would lead some people to believe that he was a spirit of God and not human. His divine nature led to precisely this problem later. Also, the "Son of God" was used formerly as a title by kings who believed they were carrying out the will of God in their rule. They were temporal rulers whereas Christ was the "spirit of God" and his sonship was in perfection and spirituality.

"And a leper came to him beseeching him, and kneeling, said to him, 'If you will, you can make me clean.' Moved with pity, he stretched out his hand and touched him, and said to him, 'I will; be clean.' And immediately the leprosy left him, and he was made clean." (Mark I: 40-42.)

The direct command of Christ's authority is evident here in nearly all the miracles involving healing. In the others the faith of the person has been referred to — faith in God being required for a person to be receptive to divine healing. In other words, one must believe in God and be willing to be obedient to his will, so that His will heals. Thus healing involves willingness and free will as well as physical healing.

The biology of healing involves life science and biological processes under the control of God, through His creative evolution. The nature of these processes, involving DNA, RNA and protein, are akin to creation of life. Healing is similar to creation biologically and biochemically. It is divine, Christian and medical.

"And when he returned to Caphernaum after some days, it was reported that he was at home. And many were gathered together, so that there was no longer room for them, not even about the door; and he was preaching the word to them; and they came, bringing to him a paralytic carried by four men. And when they could not get near him because of the crowd, they removed the roof above him; and when they had made an opening, they let down the pallet on which the paralytic lay. And when Jesus saw their faith, he said to the paralytic, 'My Son, your sins are forgiven.' Now some of the scribes were sitting there, questioning in their hearts, 'Why does this man speak thus? It is blasphemy. Who can forgive sins but God alone?' And immediately Jesus, perceiving in his spirit that they thus questioned within themselves, saith to them, 'Why do you question thus in your hearts? Which is easier to say to the paralytic, "Your sins are forgiven," or to say, "Rise, take up your pallet and walk"? But that you may know that the son of man has authority on earth to forgive sin,' he said to the paralytic, 'I say to you, rise take up your pallet and go home,' and he rose, and immediately took up the pallet and went out before them all; so that they were all amazed and glorifed God, saying, 'We never saw anything like this.' " (Mark II: 1-12.)

Jesus' miracles are evidence of the divine nature of the spirit. If it is accepted that Jesus performed miracles, then his claim to forgive sin is presumably justified. This claim in itself is clearly one of having divine nature. If the reader doubts the miracles in the bible, then recent ones by Our Lord's mother in Cairo should be considered (Chapter 9).

" 'Why does he eat with tax collectors and sinners?' And when Jesus heard it, he said to them, 'Those who are well have no need of a physician, but those who are sick, I came not to call the righteous but sinners." The emphasis here, as in Christianity in general, is on human imperfection and the need for healing and salvation. And whenever the unclean spirits beheld him, they fell down before him and cried out, "You are the Son of God." And he strictly ordered not to make him known (III: 2).

Scepticism concerning the phrase "Son of God" may be alleviated by the interpretation in a spiritual sense. Only in spirituality does perfection exist; the perfection of Christ is to be understood in this sense, and thus the term "Son of God." Its misinterpretation by non-Christians is unfortunate and should be countered by explanation.

"And there was a woman who had a flow of blood for twelve years and who had suffered much under many physicians, and had spent all that she had, and was no better but rather grew worse. She had heard the reports about Jesus, and came up behind him in the crowd and touched his garment. For she said, 'If I touch even his garments, I shall be made well.' And immediately the hemorrhage ceased; and she felt in her body that she was healed of her disease. And Jesus perceiving in himself that power had gone forth from him, immediately turned about in the crowd, and said, 'Who touched my garments?' And his disciples said to him, 'You see the crowd pressing around you, and yet you say, "Who touched me?" ' And he looked around to see who had done it, but the woman knowing what had been done to her, came in fear and trembling and fell down before him, and told him the whole truth, and he said to her, 'Daughter, your faith has made you well; go in peace, and be healed of your disease.' " (Mark V: 25-34.)

This incident is sometimes misunderstood, and it is argued that the woman's confidence cured her. The meaning which fits the gospel is that she had faith in divine power and was thus amenable to its healing quality.

"And they brought to him a man who was deaf and had an impediment in his speech; and they besought him to lay his hand upon him. And taking him aside from the multitude privately, he put his fingers into his ears, and he spat and touched his tongue: and looking up to heaven he sighed and said to him, 'Ephphatha,' that is, 'Be opened,' and his ears were opened, his tongue was released, and he spoke plainly, and he charged them to tell no one; but the more he charged them, the more zealously they proclaimed it. And they were astonished beyond measure saying, 'He has done all things well; he even makes the deaf hear and the dumb speak.' " (Mark VII: 32-37.)

In saying, "Be opened," Christ did not ask God, his spiritual Father, to cure the deaf man. He cured him on his own authority, by the spirit of God which was in him.

"And Pharisees came up and in order to test him asked, 'Is it lawful for a man to divorce his wife?' He answered them, 'What did Moses command you?' They said, 'Moses allowed a man to write with a certificate of divorce, and to put her away.' But Jesus said to them, 'For your hardness of heart he wrote you this commandment. But from the beginning of creation, God made them male and female. For this reason a man shall leave his father and mother and be joined to his wife, and the two shall become one. So they are no longer two but one. What therefore God had joined together, let no man put asunder.' And in the house the disciples asked him again about this matter — and he said to them, 'Whoever divorces his wife and marries another, commits adultery against her; and if she divorces her husband and marries another, she commits adultery.' " (Mark X: 2-12.)

Perfection is the ideal in this attitude to divorce. Christ indicates that no man shall put asunder a marriage, and still obey God's primary law. Legislation of man, i.e. politics, is a different affair, and not the business of Christianity. It is conceded that divorce does occur. From a biological viewpoint perfection is an ideal to be understood and aimed at. In politics the primary objective is humanitarian and temporary so that divorce may be expedient. Ideally, an unsuited man and woman should not marry. The basis for divorce is often adultery, in the first place, and divorce, as such, does not justify adultery, nor does it solve a problem caused by wrong. The character of man or nature of man, his form of consciousness, attachment to self and to material desires are responsible, as in marriage (as elsewhere), for much of human suffering. This includes the psychological suffering of an unsatisfactory marriage. Divorce, especially where easily obtainable, causes considerable unhappiness. Easy availability of divorce leads to lowering of moral standards.

"And as he was setting out on his journey, a man ran up and knelt before him, and asked him, 'Good Teacher, what must I do to inherit eternal life?' And Jesus said to him, 'Why do you call me good? No one is good but God alone. You know the commandments. Do not kill, do not defraud, honor your father and mother.' And he said to him, 'Teacher, all these I have observed from my youth.' And Jesus, looking upon him, loved him, and said to him, 'You lack one thing, go sell what you have, and give to the poor, and you will have treasure in heaven, and come, follow me.' At that saying his countenance fell, and he went away sorrowful; for he had great possessions.

"And Jesus looked around and said to his disciples, 'How hard it will be for those who have riches to enter the kingdom of God.' And the disciples were amazed at his words. But Jesus said to them again, 'Children, how hard it is for those who trust in riches to enter the kingdom of God. It is easier for a camel to go through the eye of a needle than for a rich man to enter the kingdom of God.' " (Mark X: 17-25.)

The reference to goodness or perfection, "No one is good but God alone," seems to imply the questioner is ascribing a character of God (perfection) to Christ. Christ's advice to "sell what you have and give to the poor" is echoed elsewhere by "Give to Caesar the things that are Caesar's and to God those that are God's," and also "You cannot serve God and mammon." The separateness of Christianity from politics and from worldly or material things is clear. Christianity is about spiritual perfection, religion and God — not materialism. In this sense it may be said to be a pure religion, unconnected directly with politics, rules, laws and primarily human values. It is about perfection. It is based on unselfishness, abolishment of suffering and healing.

"And they were on the road, going up to Jerusalem, and Jesus was walking ahead of them; and they were amazed, and those who followed were afraid, and taking the twelve again, he began to tell them what was to happen to him, saying, 'Behold, we are going to Jerusalem, and the Son of man will be delivered to the chief priests and the scribes, and they will condemn him to the Gentiles, and they will mock him and spit upon him, and scourge him, and kill him; and after three days he will rise.' " (X: 32-34.)

This is the third time that Jesus speaks about his death. There are some who suggest that such statements as this were written by Mark (and Matthew and Luke) as an afterthought, with intent to pretend prophecy. Such a suggestion may seem reasonable to one without knowledge, but study of Christianity as a whole shows the fraud has no part in its teaching. Mark had ample opportunity to hear Christ, being his contemporary, a close friend of Peter and living in Jerusalem.

"And they sent to him one of the Pharisees and some of the Herodians, to entrap him in his talk. And they came and said to him, 'Teacher we know that you are true, and care for no man; for you do not regard the position of men, but truly teach the way of God. Is it lawful to pay taxes to Caesar, or not? Should we pay them or should we not?' But knowing their hypocrisy, he said to them, 'Why put me to the test?' Jesus said to them, 'Render to Caesar the things that are Caesar's, and to God the things that are God's.' And they were amazed at him." (Mark XII: 13-17.)

The statement "you do not regard the position of men, but truly teach the way of God" is a summary of Christianity, in its essential feature. That "they were amazed at him" indicates the shock of hearing him imply separation of spirituality from politics. The innovation, for the Pharisees, was amazing because of the close involvement of religion and politics in the Middle East in the Old Testament.

"And one of the scribes came up and heard them disputing with one another, and seeing that he answered them well, asked him, 'Which commandment is the first of all?' Jesus answered, 'The first is, "Hear O Israel; The Lord our God, the Lord is one: and you shall love the Lord your God and with all you heart, and with all your soul, and with all your mind, and with all your strength." The second is this, "You shall love your neighbor as yourself." There is no other commandment greater than these.' " (Mark XII: 28-31.)

"The Lord is One" means united, undivided. The number "one" as such is not used in the gospels. God should not be referred to by a number one, or any other, since He is infinite or absolute. The Christian Trinity does not say three divisions or three Gods, but three characteristics or personalities; one cannot divide the "being" formed of the essence of perfection and truth. At the same time we can understand only by human terms and elsewhere it is implied that the perfection in the being of Christ is (part of) the perfection of God. Denials of the Trinity are vague. If they were specific in meaning these denials would be discussed rationally. There have been many "trinities," the one in the Koran apparently including Mary, mother of Jesus.

"And as they were eating, he took bread, and blessed and broke it, and gave it to them, and said, 'Take, this is my body.' And he took a cup, and when he had given thanks, he gave it to them, and they all drank of it. And he said to them, 'This is my blood of the covenant, which is poured out for many.' " (Mark XIV: 22-24.)

An understanding of the bread and wine becoming the body and blood of Christ is proposed as follows: Christ is speaking of the invisible, the "essence," the supernatural spirit. This spiritual part of life was directed into the bread and the "essence" of his blood into the wine. The essence is part of being which is invisible and supernatural and it can move independently of the body. Incidentally, our eyes can only see

186

less than one percent of what exists (in particulate and wave form). The spirit or essence of being is not visible.

"Again the high priest asked him, 'Are you the Messiah, the Son of the Blessed?' and Jesus said, 'I am; and you will see the Son of man sitting at the right hand of the Almighty, and coming with the clouds of heaven.' " (Mark XIV: 61-62.)

Some ask why Christ did not claim sooner that he was the "Son of God" (spiritually). If he had done so, he would have been executed sooner, before finishing his mission. It is quite clear in his answer "I am." Also, he uses the phrase "Son of man" to describe his other nature, which was human. Much of the misunderstanding between Islam and Christianity could be cleared up if this dual nature is accepted, and if it is clear which is being discussed in the different section of scripture.

The (spiritual) sonship of God, i.e. his special and unique spiritual relation to God, and the Christian form of the Trinity are implied by the first Gospel, that by Mark. The proposal that Christian doctrines depended on later writings such as John's Gospel or Paul's writings is contradicted by Mark's Gospel. The third personification of the Trinity is the Holy Spirit which is the spirit of God appearing on various occasions in time, in visible form.

"And they crucified him and divided his garment among them, casting lots for them, to decide what each should take. And it was the third hour, when they crucified him." (Mark XV: 24-25.)

Mark's mother witnessed the crucifixion and death of Jesus.

There is an apparent contradiction of Christ's death on the Cross in the Koran.

"That they said (in boast) 'We killed Christ Jesus, the Son of Mary, the Apostle of God' — but they killed him not, nor crucified him, but so it was made to appear to them, and those who differ therein are full of doubts, with no (certain) knowledge. But only conjecture to follow, for of a surety they killed him not." (Koran IV: 157.)

It is apparently a question of meaning, if we wish to accept the Koran and the Gospels. It may be said:

(1) Jesus did not die on the Cross;

(2) Jesus died on the Cross.

The background of theories and heresies is caused by the dual nature of Christ. Thus he was son of man and spirit of God. He died as a man. He did not die (being eternal) as spirit of God. The St. Barnabas Gospel, written about 500 A.D. against a background of heresies, contains an implication written to support Judas' substitution for Christ in the crucifixion. Barnabas' Gospel is accepted as a forgery by all Christian authorities.

"And when the sixth hour had come, there was darkness over the whole land until the ninth hour. And at the ninth hour Jesus cried with a loud voice, 'Eloi, Eloi, lama sabach thani?' which means, 'My God, My God, why has thou forsaken Me?' And Jesus uttered a loud cry and breathed his last." (Mark XV: 33-34.)

This saying of Christ is entirely compatible with his crucifixion, as a man, and supports the implication that he suffered. His suffering and death were human, the eternal nature and immortality of His spirit divine. The exclamation "My God, My God" is of a spiritual "son" to a "father." It is sometimes used by Moslems in an attempt to "disprove" the divinity of Christ. Christians, however, do not claim that Christ is God the Father, or Creator. He spoke as a spiritual Son of God.

"Afterwards he appeared to the eleven themselves as they sat at tables and he upbraided them for their unbelief and hardness of heart, because they had not believed those who saw him after he had risen. And he said to them, 'Go into the whole world and preach the gospel to the whole creation. He who believes and is baptized will be saved; but he that does not believe will be condemned.' " (Mark XVI: 14-15.)

The resurrection of Christ is borne out in the various accounts and supported by the four gospels. The condemnation of those who do not believe is taken to mean "pronounced to be wrong." The claims "Jesus is God" and "Jesus is not God" may both be accepted by Christians. Jesus is not God the Creator or "Father." Jesus is God, meaning, in Jesus, perfection and love are unlimited. He was forgiving to all, did not retaliate. His spirit of perfection flowed from God and was "part" of the infinite perfection that is divine. He was also divine (proceeding from God) in healing, unselfishness and non-attachment to material things.

The relation between reproduction and religion has become a center for discussion and controversy in recent years. Questions have involved contraception, abortion, divorce and normal standards. Life science involves the welfare, normality and health of a man, not only at the present time but also in the future. Government and religious policies have differed particularly on questions of abortion and contraception. Life science has "natural" built-in principles, not designed by man.

Perfection is an aim in life science and also in spirituality; there would be little point in imperfection as an aim for man. Thus, for religion or life science to countenance, promote or facilitate artificial contraception, abortion, permissive sexual behavior or divorce is inappropriate. Politics and materialism do not have the same aim of perfection; they deal purely with worldly human affairs. It is to be expected that they may adopt purely human attitudes towards these problems and being human in origin, design and aim these attitudes to reflect aims which are imperfect. They are purely humanist and materialist and aim at temporary and imperfect answers. Thus they can never hope to achieve perfect solutions, since they do not attempt to do so.

It is clear that where man has behaved contrary to the dictates of reason and conscience, he has found that purely material solutions have led to other problems. In the field of reproduction there are many who support artificial contraception and abortion. They treat symptoms and not the basis of the problem, which is lack of control by people of sexual impulse. Both spiritually and physiologically there is a need to control body functions, including eating, drinking, reproduction, etc. There appears to be no conflict in life science between design, function and control of reproductive processes. The spiritual and physiological needs are complementary. What are lacking are communication, understanding and unselfishness.

In man the reproductive behavioral and biological pattern is unique. The development of this pattern has accompanied the need in man for prolonged emotional involvement with a marriage partner because of the lengthy duration of "maturing" in human offspring. It takes longer to rear a human family because of the complexity of human life, and the education and communication involved. Also, the physiological needs of human offspring are greater because of mental development, and paternal as well as maternal guidance are necessary for psychological and mental maturity and stability. Development of intelligence and free will accompanied a change from "pre-human," instinctive, "obedient," to human and "disobedient." The "disobedient" implies development of intelligence, free will (independence of God, in decision making) and acceptance of standards in reproductive behavior in accord with design.

Eve was said to have been told by the Lord, "Thou shalt bring forth children in congenital stress!" Congenital stress has been investigated in our laboratory and an association has been found between blood levels of stress hormones (ACTH and cortisol) in late pregnancy and the duration of human labor. Our findings thus support Genesis and "original sin," i.e. psychosomatic stress resulting from human intelligence being reflected in "congenital stress."

Certain ills have resulted from excessive indulgence in intercourse and these include reproductive infections and abnormalities of growth, including cancer of the uterine cervix. Use of oral contraceptives, including oestrogens, tends to cause general and reproductive abnormalities also, including birth defects. Use of artificial contraceptives increases the incidence of breast cancer, since semen evidently contains protective hormones, against cancer of the breast. These findings encourage the promotion of rational control of human "reproductive pattern" from a biological viewpoint. Medicine is on the side of morality in the abortion issue. Abortion can lead to psychological and physical scarring, increase uterine infection and placental abnormaltiy.

Morality in reproduction is generally considered the business of individuals involved. It is also the field of life science since survival of the human species is involved. From the point of view of life science any interference with the normal function of reproduction is contrary to biological design. There is the design of creative evolution on the one hand and human desire on the other. Where they concur, in the interest of society, the procreation of children may result. When man interferes directly with the function of reproduction he is obviously acting against creation and the future of man. It is clear, however, that the individual has free will, and neither life science or religion can coerce him. Only guidance can be provided — control or force is not a function of religion or life science.

It is only by understanding human selfishness that we appreciate the viewpoint of those who advocate artificial contraception and abortion. Imperfection, intelligence and the motivation for pleasure are shared by most of the human species and the desire for perfection is not an innate part of human nature. It appears that the struggle will continue between purely human values, selfishness, ignorance and lack of consideration on the one hand and the aim of spiritual perfection on the other. This is especially to be expected in a materialist society. Spiritual values diminish in relation to man's increased attachment to sensory experience and to possessions.

Both life science and religion involve the welfare of individuals and of society. These have therefore much in common. Life science is concerned with spirituality insofar as this is related to man's consciousness, psychology, philosophy and behavior. Spirituality is related to life science in creation, in human design and in the welfare of man. Religion has been one of the main determinants of human behavior. There is a widespread human belief in a Creator and in an after-life and many "commandments" or laws are considered to have an origin from God. In fact, one of man's problems has been to determine what is God's will. It has been claimed that in the past God has communicated his will directly to man. Life Science as such cannot accept these claims without reserve.

Quite clearly the role of life science should coincide with the will and design of the creator. Where it does, man may be said to be "obedient to God." Where it does not, man is disobedient. In Islam man is described as "obedient to God"; in Christianity man is said to be "disobedient." Islam implies perfection and Christianity imperfection. There appears to be a contradiction here between two world religions. From the point of view of life science man is imperfect. This is true physically (see "Birth Defects and Their Causes"), and morally there is no individual who could justly claim to be perfect. Such a great claim sets oneself up as a human with divine character. Setting oneself up as perfect and obedient to God is human pride and the original sin of Christianity.

"Father" and "Son" are terms used in Christianity. One should examine their meaning before considering them suitable or not as terms applied to God and to Christ. Father means a male parent or an originator, a title of respect applied to clergy, a person of longest standing in a community, member of a fraternity or community of priests, or of a ruling body, also one who plans, manages, arranges. In the light of these meanings should the term be applicable to God? According to Christiantiy the answer is yes; according to Islam, no. In Islamic denial, it is evident that only the meaning of male (human) parent is denied. If we confine the meaning to this, Christians would agree. The meaning of the word Father is, however, much broader and is used by Christians as the planner and creator of mankind.

The word Son is a bone of contention between Christians and Moslems. The meaning implied should be considered. "Son" means male child or offspring (of a human father and mother). Also, disciple, descendent or one so regarded or treated, a native or inhabitant. There appears, at first, to be a direct contradiction between Christianity and Islam. However, in the Koran, the background of a denial of God's Sonship is of God's having women as wives and indulging in sexual activity. There is no question of such an implication in Christianity. The incarnation of Christ is considered to be the emanation or flowing of the spirit of God into the Virgin Mary so that Christ was the spirit of God. The spirit of God — from God — is considered divine and in human terms a "part" of the essence of God. In Islam, as in Aryanism, Christ was made instantaneously (similarly to Adam and contrary to Evolution) and therefore represented a part of direct creation, through a special act. There may not appear to be much in the difference here between these two religions. Life science does not accept instant creation of Adam or Christ.

The moral standard of life science is aimed at proper use and avoidance of abuse of biological reproductive function. It is now well known, as established by medical science, that artificial contraceptives cause tissue injury, or have side effects. They operate directly against the principles of survival which underlie reproductive processes. However well-meaning are the advocates of artificial contraception, it is clear that they reduce moral standards, increase extramarital pregnancies, advance sexually transmitted diseases and indirectly promote abortion. Thus they add decadence and human suffering in applying human materialist values, instead of spiritual values of human life as well as values for man's dignity, rationality and future development.

"Christ is a spiritual son of God." It appears that Christ may be described as "a" son of God or "the" Son of God; using "the," the meaning implies unique special, outstanding, next to God, and perfect or divine in nature. The implication that others may become "spiritual sons of God" is compatible with individuals reaching perfection. The question about the special position of Christ relates to this unique achievement, philosophy, mentality, healing, authority, perfection, love, self-sacrifice and resurrection — all combined in his supernatural degree of perfection.

CHAPTER 9

LIFE SCIENCE AND APPARITIONS

The observation of our Lord's mother by millions of people at the Church of Zietun, Cairo, from 1968 to 1970 has altered the attitude of science to apparitions. The fact that many people saw the apparitions, that they were repeated on many occasions, showed movement and variation, and were photographed, means that they could be judged and accepted on a scientific basis. Many miraculous cures were performed and confirmed by medical panels and are further evidence of the supernatural character of the apparitions. It remains to communicate the occurrence to those who have not heard about them, and to interpret the purpose of the apparitions.

The Church at Zeitun was built by a Christian who was told by the virgin Mary, in a dream, to build a church on this site, which his family owned (Khalil Ibrahim family). Khalil Lane, beside the church, is named after them. She promised she would appear later and bless the church. In the many apparitions of Mary, from 1968 to 1970, she was seen by millions of people repeatedly to be praying, smiling or in tears in front of

TABLE 7

Ancient Traditions of Virgin Mothers
and "Divine Incarnations"

Country	Virgin Mother	Incarnation
Tibet	Lhamoghiuprul	Fo
China	Mother conceived by a flash of light	Hoang Ti
	Virgin conceived by ray of starlight	Yao
	A pearl emblem of light caused conception	Yu
	Divine Intervention	Heou Tsi
	Schingmou conceived at the touch of a water flower	Miracle worker: Son
	A 'dark' virgin	Lao Tseu
Nepal	Maha-Mahai	Buddha
Siam	Virgin conceived by rays of sun	Sommonokhodom
Egypt	Isis, Virgin	Son
India	Virgin	Jaggernath
Persia	Dogdo: a heavenly light	Zoroaster
Paraguay	Virgin	Miracle Worker: Son

The ancient traditions of Virgin Mothers indicate the widespread expectation and belief in divine incarnation. The apparitions of the Virgin in Mexico and of the Virgin and Child in Cairo (1968-1970) and the associated miracles, are evidence in favor of the Christian belief and of the gospel narration of "The Flight into Egypt". According to the gospels this flight was to avoid the murder of Jesus by King Herod (Matthew 2). Mary told Bernadette Souberous, at Lourdes, that she (Mary) is the Immaculate Conception.

Figure 10

The Church in Zeitun, Cairo, where apparitions of Mary, Mother of Christ, appeared on many occasions during 1968-1970 to millions of people. This is in the area where the Holy Family arrived on the flight into Egypt.

the cross, on the roof of the church. Sometimes she was lying prostrate in front of the cross. It is apparent that Our Lord's mother was appealing to the people to follow her example in honoring Christ, and in praying to God through his intercession. It is evident that the crucifixion of Christ and his divinity are involved. The apparent differences in the basis of Christianity between Christians and Moslems are underlined. Some people clearly misinterpreted the apparitions as being primari-

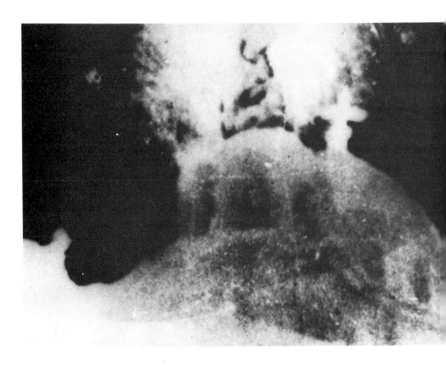

Figure 11

Apparitions at Zeitun, Cairo (1968-1970) were photographed by a number of people. The mother and child were believed to be Mary and Jesus.

ly related to the war then being fought between Egypt and Israel and to the Lord's mother taking the side of Egypt.

In Islam there is no "original sin," miracles performed by the spirit of Christ, or crucifixion and death of Jesus on the cross. Islam also apparently denies the need for Christ's redemption of man. There are denials in the Koran of the divine nature of Christ — "Jesus is not God," of the Fatherhood of God and sonship of Christ and the Trinity — in other words, of the basic themes of Christianity. It is in the light of this apparent division that we must consider the appearance and many miracles of Our Lord's Mother at Zeitun.

The appearance of Mary recalls the flight of the Holy Family (Jesus, Mary and Joseph) to Egypt, to avoid Herod's massacre of infants. This flight is referred to by Mark, in the first gospel, a few years after Christ's death. Mark lived in Jerusalem in the time of Christ and his gospel can be expected to be historically accurate.

Mary appeared on many occasions at Zeitun Church, beginning on 2nd April, 1968 and continuing until autumn 1970. Her appearance and position varied. It was often preceded by lights in the shape of doves, brilliant "clouds" of light over the church or "falling" or shooting stars. Many miraculous cures occurred to people present during apparitions at Zeitun, beginning on the first evening. These included cancers, gangrene, blindness and dumbness, paralysis, high blood pressure, heart failure, poliomyelitis, evulsion of biceps (brachialis), hernia, etc. These cures were verified by a medical committee (Papal Committee for Investigation, Report: Cairo 1969).

The following is a statement issued on 5th May 1968 by Anba Kyrillos VI, Pope of Alexandria and Patriarch of the See of St. Mark. "Since April 2nd 1968, the Apparition of the Blessed Virgin Mary has appeared several times on the Coptic Orthodox Church named after Her, at Zeitun in Cairo. The apparition has appeared during different nights and is still appearing in varying forms: sometimes in complete body and others in half, always surrounded by a white glittering halo appearing either from the dome openings or from the space between the domes on which she used to move and march and bow before the cross on the church roof, giving it a magnificent light. She used also to face multitudes of people in front of the church and bless them with her hands and with nods from her blessed head. In some other times the Apparition was in the form of a body of a celestial glittering white cloud or in the form of light preceded by some spiritual forms such as doves of great speed. The Apparition used to appear for a long period that reached in certain times two hours and a

Figure 12

Apparitions at Zeitun, Cairo (1968-1970). Mary, or "Miriam," was seen by millions of people and many were cured of serious illness.

quarter, as happened on April 30th, 1968, when her complete glittering Apparition stayed form 2:45 to 5 o'clock in the morning.

"The appearances have been witnessed by many thousands of citizens and foreigners belonging to different religions and sects, together with groups of religious organizations and scientific and professional personages and all other categories of people who have proclaimed and announced their witnesses confirming the certainty of the Virgin's appearances — all giving the same particulars as to description and form and time and place, thus proving a whole agreement in witnessing that has elevated the matter of apperance above any doubt or any lack of proof or evidence.

"These appearances have been accompanied by two important matters: The first is the vivid spirit of belief in God, the other World and the Saints; thus having many of the unbelievers and those of weak belief repent through this cause of belief. The second is the miraculous cure that has occurred to many patients whose cases have been examined by all concerned medically and scientifically.

"The Papal Residence has collected the evidence that has been looked after by authorized personalities and committees of clergymen who have been pursuing and investigating and who even had the chance to observe the blessed apparition for themselves and recording their research and witness in official reports which they submitted to His Holiness The Pope Anba Kyrillos VI.

"The Papal Residence, by issuing this statement, declares with complete faith, great rejoicing and with gratitude submitted through self-humiliation to Almighty God that the Blessed Virgin Mary has appeared several times in clear and steady forms during many different nights for varying periods that reached in some of them to more than two hours' continuity, since the 2nd of April 1968 up to now in the Coptic Orthodox Church at Zeitun, Cairo. That it is in Matariya Road through which the Holy Family has passed during their settlement in Egypt as is well-known historically.

"We hope this blessing will be a sign of peace in the world

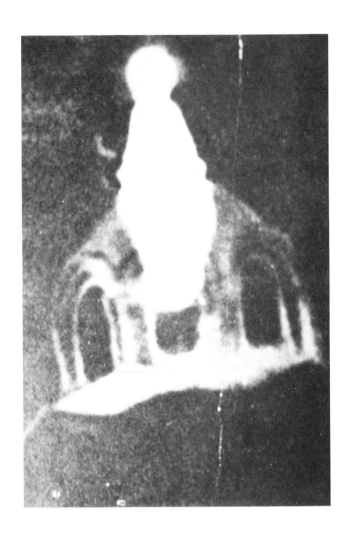

Figure 13

**Apparitions at Zeitun, Cairo (1968-1970).
Photograph of outline of Mary, or "Miriam."**

Figure 14

Apparitions at Cairo: A drawing made by an onlooker.

and an omen of prosperity to our beloved patron and blessed nation."

From the point of view of life science the third paragraph (beginning with "The appearances have witnessed") is acceptable as scientific evidence. We should note especially that the many witnesses all gave the same particulars as to description and form and time and place thus presenting a whole agreement in witnessing that has elevated the matter of appearance above any doubt or any lack of proof or evidence.

A photograph shows an imprint of the Virgin Mary, which can be seen in Mexico City, and which is scientific evidence.

Four pages — 25 milliemes

The Egyptian Gazette

ذى اجيبشيان جازيت

89th Year No. 28345 ✻   Sunday, May 5, 1968

'irgin Mary appeared at Zeitun -- Kyr

» العنوان الذى ظهر فى جريدة الاجيبشيان جازيت يوم ٥ مايو سنة ١٩٦٨ وهو

(العـذراء مريم تظهر فى الزيتون – البابا كيرلس السادس) »

Figure 15

Newspaper heading from the Egyptian Gazette of May 5, 1968. The apparitions of Mary received widespread recognition and publicity in Egypt.

The imprint is on a cloak or shawl and dates from 1531 A.D. It was a response to a request by Bishop Zumaraga for a sign from her to confirm her appearance and her request for a shrine to be built. The Virgin appeared to Juan Diego on four occasions in the same area on a hill in a suburb of Mexico City, the first being 9th December. After asking Juan where he was going she said, "Know for certain, that I am the perfect and perpetual Virgin Mary, Mother of the True God through whom everything lives, the Lord of all things near and far, the Master of Heaven and Earth.

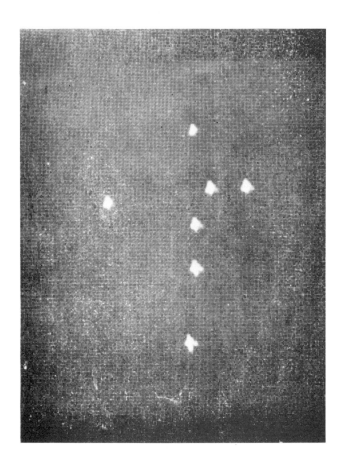

Figure 16

Doves in the shape of a cross, photographed during the apparitions in Cairo. The form presumably represents Christ, the Crucifixion and Christianity.

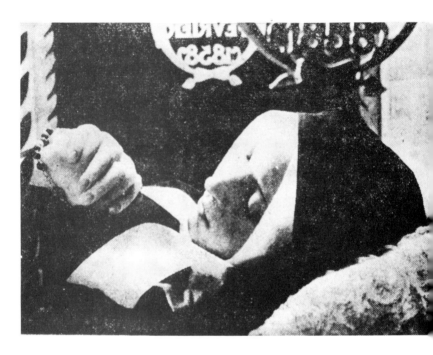

Figure 17

St. Bernadette, visionary of Lourdes, to whom Mary claimed she is the Immaculate Conception. Lifelike appearance 100 years after death.

"I wish and intensely desire that in this place my sanctuary be erected. Here I will demonstrate, I will exhibit, I will give all my love, my compassion, my help and my protection to the people. I am your merciful mother. The merciful mother of all of you who live united in this land, and of all mankind, of all those who love me, of those who cry for me, of those who seek me, of those who have confidence in me. Here I will hear their weeping, their sorrow, and will remedy, and alleviate all their multiple sufferings, necessities and misfortunes.

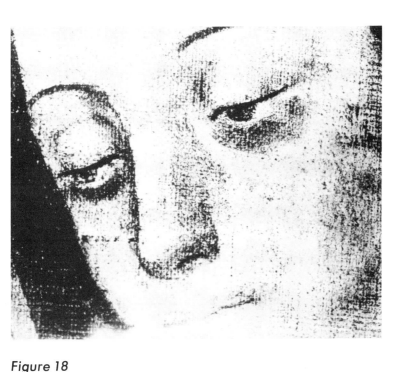

Figure 18

Mary of Guadelupe, "Mother of God." Image from cloak in Guadelupe, Mexico.

"In order that my wish may be fulfilled, you must go to Mexico, to the house of the Bishop and tell him that I sent you, that it is my desire to have a sanctuary built for me here. Tell him what you have seen and heard, and be sure I shall be grateful to you for doing what I ask. I shall make you happy and reward you for the service which you will render to me. My son, you have heard my wish. Go in peace."

At the fourth appearance the Virgin Mary asked Juan to gather flowers on the hill and bring them to her. (There were normally no flowers there in December.) She asked him to go

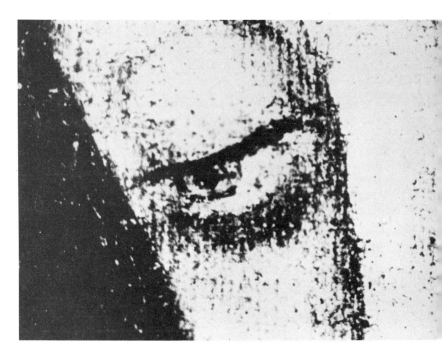

Figure 19

Eye from illustration at left. Figure of Juan Diego, to whom Mary appeared, was apparently reflected in her right eye.

to the Bishop and when he opened out his cloak, giving it to the Bishop, there was the picture of her on it.

"Thus he spread out his white mantle in which he carried the flowers and when all the different Castilian roses had cascaded to the floor, there was outlined upon it and suddenly there appeared the precious image of the Immaculate Virgin Holy Mary, Mother of God, just as it can still be seen today in her Gospel in Tepeyae."

A photograph of the Virgin's face on enlargement showed an image like that of Juan Diego on the right eye; apparently

208

his reflection. A photograph of the virgin's image and an enlargement is reproduced in this chapter.

The history of this apparition was written about 1560 by Antonio Velariano, an educated Indian who was an instructor in the Imperial College of the Holy Cross at Thaltelolco and later a Governor in the city of Mexico.

Only these two apparitions, at Guadelupe (Mexico) and Zeitun (Cairo), are described here. There is evidence that both are accurate accounts and the apparitions in Cairo were seen by many thousands of people. There are many apparitions which are not evidenced by such clear testimony as these, and for this reason they are not described here. Only those two which are definitely acceptable for scientific reasons are referred to here. It is admitted that there is evidence also for apparitions of Mary in Knock (Ireland), Lourdes (France), Fatima (Portugal) and other locations.

The vision at Knock comprised Mary, Joseph, John the Evangelist and a lamb on the altar. It was seen on August 21st, 1879 by fifteen people. John was recognized from the likeness to his statue in a church — his appearance is interpreted as supporting his gospel, which teaches the divine nature of Jesus.

At Fatima three children saw Mary — the choice of Fatima was considered to be aimed at bridging the gap between Islam and Christianity — one of Muhammed's daughters was named Fatima. The Portuguese girl called Fatima was a Muslim and became a Christian. Mary is believed to have chosen the village of Fatima because of this.